Date Due

ES YOU

Code 4386-04, CLS-4, Broadman Supplies, Nashville, Tenn.,
Printed in U.S.A.

59 Gospel Talks
for Children
to See and Hear

SMile!
GOD LOVES YOU

by
Lavern G. Franzen

AUGSBURG PUBLISHING HOUSE
MINNEAPOLIS, MINNESOTA

SMILE! GOD LOVES YOU

Contents

To my wife Mary Ann

Preface

It's not easy to be a child in church.

On the one hand is the reality of adult concerns that children be properly quiet, immobile, and attentive. On the other hand is another reality of the adult world. For a child it is a world in which pews are several sizes too large, hymns several stanzas too long, and sermon words several syllables too complex. There is little to claim a child's interest, little to attract his attention, and even little to invite his participation. The adult church offers a child little to convince him that God's love is exciting and real or that he is already a significant part of the sharing of that love.

Yet the church hopes the child is so convinced. After all, children are the church. The Christ of the adult is their Christ now, and if the gospel is "God's good news about man's bad situation" for the grown-ups, so it is for young Christians. God's people need to share it as that *good* news.

These visual messages are for children. They are drawn from those shared in the worship services of Our Redeemer congregation.

They are more than simple object lessons. Hopefully, they illustrate the law/gospel concepts essential to kerygmatic preaching. They have been used as parallels to adult messages on the same themes.

In a very practical way, these children's messages permit physical involvement in the worship service. We invite the children to move forward to the chancel steps for "their message." There is a little confusion during the movement, but this is more than offset by the physical relief such movement gives children, and by the opportunities for direct participation it affords. Our experiences tell us that such movement makes it a little easier to be a child in church.

To the members of Our Redeemer in Temple Terrace, and especially to my wife, Mary Ann, and our children Sherrie and Debbie, my thanks for their willingness to hear, experiment, criticize, improve, and above all, encourage. Ultimately, that too is gospel action, the people of God, saying to one another SMILE! GOD LOVES YOU!

LAVERN FRANZEN

What Were You Expecting?

SCRIPTURE

And when he entered Jerusalem, all the city was stirred, saying, "Who is this?" And the crowds said, "This is the prophet Jesus from Nazareth of Galilee."

Matthew 21:1, 11   (First Sunday in Advent)

PREPARATION

Prepare a set of very simple line drawings, showing the outline of the following objects: a king's crown; a sword and spear; the two tablets of the Law; a book entitled *How to Live;* a church; a cross.

When Jesus rode into Jerusalem it was a very exciting time. The people expected something great from him. They thought he would be a new king, and that he would drive out the Roman soldiers. They would have their land back again. They expected great things!

But that's also why they were disappointed with Jesus. They didn't get what they expected from him. They expected him to be like this. (Show the crown.) They probably expected him to use something like this. (Show the sword and spear.) But they were wrong, and they were disappointed. He wasn't what they expected.

People are still sometimes disappointed with Jesus. They still expect different things from him. Some think he came to give us this. (Show the set of the commandments.) That's right, they expect him to give us a new kind of law, new rules to follow, new commandments to keep. Or some think he came to do this. (Show the picture of the book with the title *How to Live.*) They think he came to be just another teacher, and nothing more. Some others think he came to do this. (Show the picture of the church building.) Yes, they think he came to start another church, and they're disappointed when the church isn't quite what they think it should be. Jesus just isn't what many people expect.

11

He didn't come for any of those things we mentioned, though. He came for something else. (Show the cross.) That's right! He came to use a cross instead of a crown or a sword. He came to keep the Law, and not to make new ones. He came to give us new life, a life that is pleasing to God.

That's even better than we expected, isn't it? That's because Jesus is always so much more than we could expect!

Time to Wake Up

SCRIPTURE

And then they will see the Son of man coming in a cloud with power and great glory. Now when these things begin to take place, look up and raise your heads, because your redemption is drawing near.

Luke 22:27, 28 (Second Sunday in Advent)

PREPARATION

The basic visual aid for this message is an alarm clock. If you can set it precisely enough so that it will interrupt your talking, do so. Otherwise, just pull the alarm button when you want it to sound.

You will also need pictures illustrating some of the events which Christ calls the signs of the times. Included could be pictures of soldiers in battle, of storms, of destruction of houses, etc. (Note: If these pictures are too gory, they may detract. It is better to err on the gentle side.)

Many of you go to school every morning, don't you? How many do? (Allow time for the children to respond.) Now, let me ask you a question. Do you wake up every morning in time for school all by yourself? Sometimes you do, I suppose, but probably not all the time. Most of you are probably like I am. I need someone or something to wake me.

That's why I need something like this. (Show the alarm clock.) You know what this is, don't you? And you know how it works. We can be sound asleep, maybe even dreaming, when all of a sudden . . . (Pull the alarm button so that the clock sounds. Continue talking until it does sound, though, so that it actually interrupts.) Just like that the alarm sounds, and we wake up. And it's a good thing we have something like alarm clocks, or we might not be ready for school. This is the signal that it's time to wake up.

Jesus tells us that he has given us some signals too, but for a different reason. He has told us that he is coming back sometime and wants us to be ready when he comes. But he didn't tell us just when. He did say that he would give us some signals, though. He said that when these things happen, they would be his signals that he will be back soon. (As you say this last sentence, show the pictures with comments for each one, or with response from the children to each one.)

But do you know something? These things are happening right now! Maybe the alarm clock is already ringing. We don't know how long Jesus will let his signals go on.

But the good thing is that we are ready right now! That's why Jesus came the first time, when he lived with people just like us. He gave us the signs of his love then, by helping people, by healing people, by suffering and dying for people. And it wasn't just for the people then that he brought his love, but for all of us. He did it to take away our sins and to fill us with love for him again. That's why we are ready for him to come again. And that's why we don't have to be afraid when he comes back. His alarm clock and his signals, are telling us that someone who loves us very much is near.

I Think Jesus Is . .

SCRIPTURE

Now when John heard in prison about the deeds of the Christ, he sent word by his disciples and said to him, "Are you he who is to come, or shall we look for another?" And Jesus answered them, "Go and tell John what you hear and see: the blind receive their sight, and the lame walk, lepers are cleansed and the deaf hear, and the dead are raised up, and the poor have good news preached to them. And blessed is he who takes no offense at me."

Matthew 11:2-6   (Third Sunday in Advent)

PREPARATION

Use either pictures collected from newspapers or magazines, or single line drawings of stick figures made with felt-tip marking pens, preferably on light cardboard. (Actually, the stick figures are preferable. They allow the young people more exercise of their imaginations, and so involve them more in the whole process.)

Picture 1: A blind person. The stick figure can show one person leading another by the hand, with the one being led holding a cane. The second part of this picture can show the person throwing the cane away.

Picture 2: A deaf person. The stick picture can show a person shouting into the ear of another. The second picture in the sequence can show two people speaking normally.

Picture 3: A crippled person. The stick figure can be a person walking with aid of crutches. The other one in the sequence can show him walking normally.

Picture 4: A tombstone. The first picture can show just the grave marker. The second one can show a person standing alongside it.

Picture 5: A cross.

Picture 6: A baptismal font or baptismal shell.

When Jesus came to the world many years ago, people didn't know exactly what to think of him. God had sent John the Baptizer to help people get ready for Jesus, but even John wasn't always sure. So he sent some of his students to Jesus to ask "Are you the one who is to come?"

Jesus said "Tell John what you see." And here are the things he told them to look at.

(Show picture one, and provide for discussion and response. Continue with each picture through picture number four. After all have been discussed briefly, summarize and continue.)

Well, what did they see? They saw Jesus healing the blind, the deaf, the cripples, and even the dead. What do you think John's students said when they went back? Was Jesus the one they were watching for? Of course he was!

He gives us something to watch for too. (Show the cross.) Really, this is the way he heals us. When we're so blind we can't see our sins (cover eyes with hands); or so deaf (cover ears) that we don't want to hear about them; or so lame with sin (bend over) that we can't live like God's people ought to live, Jesus comes to us. This is his sign. (Show cross again.) It's the sign of his love for us and his forgiveness to us. It means that we can see, we can hear, and we aren't lame Christians after all. We're his people. We can even say he raised us from being dead, too. (Show font or shell.) That happened when we were baptized. He came to us then, and made his sign over us. He has been watching over us, and we can watch for him!

What's a Church, Anyway?

SCRIPTURE

For where two or three are gathered in my name, there am
I in the midst of them.

Matthew 18:20   (Fourth Sunday in Advent)

PREPARATION

The visual aids for this message will be a collection of pictures. You will need several pictures of churches of varying
styles, a picture of a Bible, a picture of a baptismal font, and
a picture of a chalice or a communion set. (Excellent sources
for such pictures are ecclesiastical arts catalogues, publishing
house catalogues, or church building magazines.)

If you choose, simple line drawings will also serve instead
of the pictures suggested.

I know all of you will be able to answer my first question today. The question is "Where are you?" That's an
easy one, isn't it? You're at church. Everybody knows
that.

But now let's ask another question. What is a church?
Is this a church? (Show first picture.) How do you
know? (Allow time for response.) How about this one?
Is this a church? (Again allow time for response.) Well,
is this one a church? How do you know it is? (Repeat
the procedure established with the first two pictures.)

Now I'm going to surprise you. You said all those
pictures were pictures of churches. But do you know
something? They're not, not really. They are church
buildings. Do you know what a church is? A church is
people. The building is simply the place they come to
do what the church does.

So really, we should ask what the church does. That's
a better question than what does a church look like,
anyway. And here's what the church does. (Show Bible.)
It gathers to share the word of God. (Show baptismal
font.) It baptizes people. (Show chalice.) It celebrates

communion. Where those things happen, there is the church.

It's just as Jesus said. Where two or three are gathered in his name, there he is in the midst of them.

So, what is a church? (Point to walls.) This is a church building. But you're the church. Jesus is with you and with all the people here today.

Wrapped Up Like Us

SCRIPTURE

And she gave birth to her first-born son and wrapped him in swaddling cloths, and laid him in a manger, because there was no place for him in the inn.

Luke 2:7 (Christmas Day)

PREPARATION

Wrap the infant and manger from a small creche set in Christmas gift wrap, preferably one which has Santa Claus figures on it. If this is not available, substitute by using Santa Claus stickers. Use a decorative ribbon and bow to complete the package.

Today is Christmas Day and what an exciting time it is. After all, we've been waiting for it to come, haven't we? And we've been busy buying presents, wrapping them, and giving them. Today, we've been busy unwrapping them, too, haven't we? It's really an exciting day.

So, I'm excited too. Just look. I have a Christmas present I haven't even unwrapped yet. Look at the pretty ribbon, and at this nice bow, and even at the wrapping paper. There's a picture of Santa Claus on it, and he is fun to think about, isn't he? And there are other fun things about Christmas, too. There's the Christmas tree and the cookies and the candy and everything like that. There is so much to think about!

But that's why we have to be careful, too. Sometimes those things can be more important for us than anything else. Sometimes they can seem like the real reason we have Christmas.

You would think I was silly if I decided I liked this package so much I wouldn't even open it to see what was inside, wouldn't you? It would be funny if all I wanted was the ribbon and the bow and wrapping paper, and would miss out on the real gift. It's funny, too—but sort of sad—if we get all excited about everything else in Christmas and miss out on the real gift. The tree and the candy and the cookies and the presents are like the ribbons and wrapping; the real gift is something else.

So, maybe we should open this gift. (Do so.)

Now what do I have? What was my gift? That's right; it's the baby Jesus, reminding us how he came at Christmas. He was all wrapped up, too, not in ribbons and bows and Christmas paper, but in a baby's body, to be just like us. That's what Christmas is really all about. Jesus wrapped himself up like one of us, to bring God's love to us and to take our sins from us. And he still comes to us with that love, wrapping it in the water of our baptism, and in the ribbon of his word, and even in the package of his body and blood in communion. That's the exciting thing about Christmas. It's not our wrapping but God's gift!

Peace!

SCRIPTURE

Lord, now lettest thou thy servant depart in peace, according to thy word; for mine eyes have seen thy salvation. . . .

Luke 2:29, 30 (Sunday after Christmas)

PREPARATION

On the upper half of a piece of heavy paper or light cardboard print the word *SHALOM* in heavy letters; below it, in such a way that the paper can be folded to cover it, print the word *PEACE*. On the reverse side, print the word *SHALOM* also, with a very bold heavy line cross running through the exact center of it. Now cut the paper so that the cross is divided, part on each side.

This morning we're going to learn a new word. It's the word you see on this paper. It's pronounced shah-lohm. Let's all say it together, so that we know it. (Have children repeat the word until most of them are able to say it.) That's good! Now we can say the word. Of course, we ought to know what it means, too. It means this: (Uncover the bottom of the paper, still holding the parts together, to show the word *PEACE*.)

That's right. Shalom means peace. It means wholeness; it means things being together. That's peace. When you and your friend are playing together, having fun, that's peace; that's shalom. Or when you and your brother are working together to mow the lawn, that's shalom. You're at peace.

But we know that we aren't always such peaceful people, are we? We get angry with each other, and we're really not together anymore. (Pull halves of the paper apart from each other.) Then we don't have peace; we have separation. Or sometimes we quarrel or become jealous. (Pull the pieces of paper farther apart.) Our shalom is broken; we don't have peace. That happens between people, between parents, between those of different colors, even between countries. Instead of being together we are apart; instead of shalom we have trouble. Instead of peace, we have fighting. Instead of peace with God, we have sin.

And that's the reason Jesus came. He came to be the Prince of Peace, as the Bible calls him. He came to bring people back together again, to bring them together with God, and to bring them together with each other. (Turn paper so reverse shows, moving halves toward each other, until they join.) And do you see how he did it? He did it with his cross. He came to take our sins away, our sins of being angry or jealous or hateful, our sins of separating ourselves from each other. He came to fill us with his love, and to wash away our sins and our separation with his forgiveness. He came to live in us, and he is the Prince of Peace. He has brought us back to God, and he brings us back to each other. (Move paper apart, but then bring the paper halves together again.) He came so that we can live in shalom. That means peace.

Don't Get Squeezed In!

SCRIPTURE

Do not be conformed to this world but be transformed by the renewal of your mind.

Romans 12:2   (First Sunday after Epiphany)

PREPARATION

You will need a box with a cover. This box must be large enough so that you can squeeze a small doll into it, but small enough so that the doll must be squeezed into it. On one end of the box staple or tape a paper with the words *anger, jealousy, disobeying, cheating, lying.* On the other end, attach another paper of the same size with the words *love, kindness, obedience, honesty, truth.* In the box place a cross.

When people live without Jesus and his word, it's very easy for them to live just for themselves. On the front of this box are some things that show it . . . things like being angry, being jealous, disobeying parents or teachers, cheating, lying, and we could name others. There are things like being selfish, or always trying to get even, or staying away from Sunday school or church.

We know all those things are wrong, but we know they happen. They happen when people live without Jesus, but sadly, they happen to us, too. We do the same things people without Jesus do. We're getting squeezed into their box. (Squeeze doll down into box, and close the cover. Be certain that the list of sins is toward the group.) And that's not a very good life, to be squeezed in that way.

But we don't have to be! Jesus came to change all that. He came to give us new life, by lifting us out of the box, and even by changing it around for us. He took off the lid of our sins. (Lift cover from box, and lift doll out. Then turn the box around so the Christian qualities show.) Instead of being angry we can love each other. Instead of being squeezed into the sins of jealousy or

23

disobedience or selfishness or lying, we are rescued from them. Jesus came to lift us out. We aren't squeezed in any more. We're free. He has rescued us.

That's exactly what happened, in fact. Jesus came to the world to rescue it. Sin was squeezing it away from God, but he "squeezed" himself into the world as a little baby. He let himself be "squeezed" on the cross by angry, jealous, selfish people. (Show the cross.) He even let himself be "squeezed" into the grave. But he didn't stay there. He came out, and now he comes to us. He sets us free with his love and his forgiveness. We have his power, and we're not squeezed in any more!

Love Means Helping

SCRIPTURE

If we live by the Spirit, let us also walk by the Spirit. Let us have no self-conceit, no provoking of one another, no envy of one another.

Brethren, if a man is overtaken in any trespass, you who are spiritual should restore him in a spirit of gentleness. Look to yourselves, lest you too be tempted. Bear one another's burdens, and so fulfil the law of Christ.

Galatians 5:25-6:2 (Second Sunday after Epiphany)

PREPARATION

Fill a suitcase with heavy objects, such as books or bricks. Place it along one side of the room, where the child carrying it will have some distance to transport it.

This morning I need someone to help me. Who would like to? (Allow time for the children to volunteer. Then choose one of the smallest ones, someone obviously too small to handle the suitcase you have prepared.) I'm glad so many want to help. I think I'll ask Mary to help today. Mary, would you please bring me that suitcase by the side of the room? (Wait for Mary to get the suitcase. As soon as she tries to lift it, continue, addressing her.)

What's the problem, Mary? Is it too heavy? Well, maybe we need one or two more. (Choose two others, this time picking someone strong enough to carry the case.) Robert and Ronnie, will you please help, too? (Wait until they get to the suitcase, and have them bring it to you.)

That was much easier, wasn't it? It was just too heavy for Mary to lift alone. And Mary, if you knew what was in the suitcase, you'd know why. I filled it with bricks, just to make it very heavy. That way we could see that we would have to have some help. This teaches us something about love, because love means helping.

25

Of course, sometimes it seems we don't like to help each other. If someone does something wrong, we make fun of him, or tell others about him. We criticize each other, or find fault with each other, or think we're better than one another. That doesn't show much love, does it? That's not helping at all.

But that's why Jesus came. He came to take those sins, too. He loved us so much that he came to be our helper. And for him helping us meant taking away all our sins, and giving us his strength when we need it. We don't have to criticize each other or make fun of one another or tell on each other. Jesus took those sins away. We can love one another, and we can help each other. Jesus has rescued us from thinking only about ourselves, or from thinking too highly of ourselves. That's the way he helps us; that's the way we start helping others.

Here's a Better Way

SCRIPTURE

Live in harmony with one another; do not be haughty, but associate with the lowly; never be conceited. Repay no one evil for evil, but take thought for what is noble in the sight of all. If possible, so far as it depends on you, live peaceably with all. Beloved, never avenge yourselves, but leave it to the wrath of God; for it is written, "Vengeance is mine, I will repay, says the Lord." No, "if your enemy is hungry, feed him; if he is thirsty, give him drink; for by so doing, you will heap burning coals upon his head." Do not be overcome by evil, but overcome evil with good.

Romans 12:16-21   (Third Sunday after Epiphany)

PREPARATION

Since this is an action response, there will be no materials necessary.

This morning I'm going to ask all of you to help me. I'm going to ask you to do certain things. Are we all ready?

First, show me what you would do when I do this. (Smile broadly at the group.) That's right; you would do the same thing, wouldn't you? If I smile at you, you will probably smile at me. Our smiles show that we like each other.

But now, show me what you would do if I do this. (Make a fist, and shake it at the children.) Things are much different now, aren't they? I didn't see any smiles this time. Some of you looked afraid, and I think some of you might have been looking for a place to hide. One or two of you even made fists yourselves; you must have wanted to protect yourselves.

Now what if I do this? (Aim a punch at one of the boys, but pull it back before it hits him.) You did something very natural, didn't you? You ducked! Of course you did; you didn't want to get hit. And if you were big enough, you probably would make your own fist and try to hit back. That's the way we are. We like to get even with each other.

But Jesus has given us a better way . . . a better way than getting even. Jesus tells us to love our enemies, and even to help them. If they are hungry, he says, we ought to feed them. Or if they are thirsty, we ought to give them something to drink. That's better than getting even.

But Jesus not only told us to do that, he did it himself. He loved his enemies, and even asked God to forgive those who were crucifying him. He loves us, and with our sins we could say we are enemies of God. But he feeds us with his love, and lets us drink of his forgiveness. He didn't come to get even with us, but to help us. And that's the way he still comes to us, to live in us with a better way to treat people. We don't have to get even. Jesus lives in us, and we can give his love to others.

Taking Out the Wrinkles

SCRIPTURE

. . and any other commandments are summed up in this sentence, "You shall love your neighbor as yourself." Love does no wrong to a neighbor; therefore love is the fulfilling of the law.

Romans 13:9, 10 (Fourth Sunday after Epiphany)

PREPARATION

From red construction paper cut out two hearts, making each at least six inches in height. You will also need a cross, preferably four or five inches or more.

All of you know what I have in my hand this morning, don't you. (Elicit answers from the children. You will probably be told that you hold a valentine, a heart, etc.) But I wonder if you know what this means? (Again, allow the children to respond, until you get the answer "Love.") That's right, a heart means love! When we send a valentine to someone, it's a way of saying we love that person. That's why valentines are such fun to send or to get. It's good to love people, and to know that others love us.

And God tells us that is the way his people are to live. They are to love each other, to have loving hearts for one another. (Hold up a heart as if to demonstrate.)

The problem is that we just aren't perfect people, and we don't love each other perfectly, either. We get angry with our brothers or sisters, and our love isn't perfect then. (Crumple heart slightly.) Or we quarrel with our friends, and it's not so perfect then either. (Crumple it more.) We disobey our parents. (Crumple it still more.) We fight with our schoolmates, or say bad things about someone in our class. (Crumple the heart more with each statement, until it is completely crumpled.)

But look what has happened to our heart. (Show it.)

It's all crumpled up, all wrinkled. We just couldn't ever get it straightened out.

That is, *we* couldn't. But Jesus did. He brought God's love to us, and that's a perfect love. There are no wrinkles in his love at all. He showed his love with this. (Show the cross.) And that's even better than showing it with a heart. Do you know why? Because with this (show the cross) Jesus has the power to smooth all the wrinkles out of this. He took away all the sins which crumple our hearts. He takes out all the rough places in our love with his forgiveness, and he gives us new hearts to love one another again. (Show the new heart.) That really is good news! Just think, the wrinkles are gone. Jesus takes them away. So, look at the person next to you! You can love him with a new heart. Jesus gave it to you!

Our New Clothes

SCRIPTURE

> Put on then, as God's chosen ones, holy and beloved, compassion, kindness, lowliness, meekness, and patience, forbearing one another and, if one has a complaint against another, forgiving each other; as the Lord has forgiven you, so you must also forgive. And above all these put on love, which binds everything together in perfect harmony. And let the peace of Christ rule in your hearts, to which indeed you were called in the one body.
>
> Colossians 3:12-15   (Fifth Sunday after Epiphany)

PREPARATION

> The visual aid for this message is a paper doll with several sets of clothes, and a marking pen. (The larger the paper doll, the better.)

I'd like you to meet my friend this morning. I'm going to call her Sally. Actually, though, I could call her any name; I could even call her any of your names. And if I had a boy doll, I could call him any of the boy's names, too. You see, I want you to pretend that this is really every one of us, and not just Sally at all.

But I want you to notice something. Sally has a bright new dress, a very pretty one. She was wearing this dress when she was playing with her friend, Mary. But something very sad happened. Mary stepped on Sally's dress when she was kneeling down, and just a tiny little bit tore. Mary felt so sorry, and it was an accident. But Sally became very angry. Even when Mary wanted to have her mother sew the tiny tear, Sally became more angry than ever. (Write the word *ANGER* across part of the dress.) She even told Mary "I hate you!" (Write the word *HATE* across the dress.) And then she said "And I'll never, never forgive you, either!" (Write the word *UNFORGIVING* across the dress.)

Now all of that really spoiled Sally's dress, didn't it? It's not nearly so pretty now.

And that's the way our lives are spoiled, too. God tells us that we are to be kind to one another, but we get just as angry as Sally. (Underline ANGER.) He tells us that we are to love each other, but we often hate. (Underline HATRED.) He tells us that he has forgiven us, so we should forgive others, but we refuse to. (Underline UNFORGIVING.) We just make our clothes dirtier and dirtier, and if our sins against each other were written on our clothes, the way I wrote these on Sally's, we wouldn't be very pretty people at all.

But that's why God sent Jesus to us. He didn't want his people to be all covered up with their sins. Instead he covers us with bright new clothes of his forgiveness for us. He took our sins as his very own, so that we could have clean new robes, as the Bible says. If I only had a very good eraser I could show you by taking the marks off Sally's dress. That's what Jesus does for us; he takes off the marks, and puts new clothes on us, instead. Maybe I can show it this way. (Put new dress on the doll.) That's the way we are! That's the way Jesus makes us.

God-in-a-Box

SCRIPTURE

And after six days Jesus took with him Peter and James and John his brother, and led them up a high mountain apart. And he was transfigured before them, and his face shone like the sun, and his garments became white as light. And behold, there appeared to them Moses and Elijah, talking with him. And Peter said to Jesus, "Lord, it is well that we are here; if you wish, I will make three booths here, one for you and one for Moses and one for Elijah." He was still speaking when lo, a bright cloud overshadowed them, and a voice from the cloud said, "This is my beloved Son, with whom I am well pleased; listen to him."

Matthew 17:1-5   (Transfiguration Sunday)

PREPARATION

Prepare a cardboard box so that the cover can be removed A shoe box will serve well.

All of you can see that I have a box in my hands this morning. But I don't think anyone knows what I have in my box. It looks like a shoe box, doesn't it? But I have something else in it. Know what that is? (Open box and peek in, exaggerating the action of keeping the contents secret from the children.) Nobody knows what I have in my box! (Open it again, repeating the action.) Would you like to know? I'll tell you! I have God in my box! (Allow a little time for this to register.)

That's right! I have God in my box! Now would you like to see? (Open box so that the children can see.) What do you see? (Wait for an answer.) That's right! You see nothing! And do you know why? It's because there is nothing there. You see, I was only teasing when I said I had God in my box. We all know that we can't keep God in a box, don't we?

But it's funny, we sometimes try, anyway. Peter wanted Jesus to stay on the mountaintop with him so that he wouldn't have to go to Jerusalem and suffer and die. That's like keeping God in a box. Or when we think that it's so nice to love and pray to God here, but forget him everyplace else, that's keeping him here in a box. Or even when we talk in church about loving all people, but then don't show that love to others who are with us in school or on the playground, we're keeping God in a box.

But God isn't a God-in-a-box, at all. And he won't let us keep him there. He's alive wherever we are. He did send Jesus to be boxed into our world, but Jesus didn't stay boxed in. We could even say that when he was crucified, he was put into something like a box. But he didn't stay in that, either. He wouldn't stay on the mountain with Peter, he didn't stay in his grave. And he won't be kept in our box either.

But that's really good news for us. Jesus won't stay in a box of any kind . . . not this one (show box) or in the bigger one. (Indicate the church.) He is alive in the whole world. That means we don't have to stay in the box to be with him, either, but wherever we are, he is with us, sharing his power and his love. He's not a God-in-a-box.

Come, Mow My Lawn

SCRIPTURE

". . . And when evening came, the owner of the vineyard said to his steward, 'Call up the laborers and pay them their wages, beginning with the last, up to the first.' And when those hired about the eleventh hour came, each of them received a denarius. Now when the first came, they thought they would receive more; but each of them also received a denarius. And on receiving it they grumbled at the householder, saying, 'These last worked only one hour, and you have made them equal to us who have borne the burden of the day and the scorching heat.' But he replied to one of them, 'Friend, I am doing you no wrong; did you not agree with me for a denarius? Take what belongs to you, and go; I choose to give to this last as I give to you. Am I not allowed to do what I choose with what belong to me? Or do you begrudge my generosity?' So the last will be first and the first last."

Matthew 20:8-16 (Septuagesima Sunday)

PREPARATION

Make three clock faces, showing the hands in 8:00 o'clock, 12:00 o'clock, and 4:00 o'clock positions respectively. Also have three one-dollar bills available.

Some of you boys mow lawns, don't you? (Substitute shovel sidewalks if that is more appropriate.) Well, this morning let's pretend that my lawn needs mowing, and so I'd like to hire someone to do it. I'd like you to start early tomorrow morning, and of course I'll pay you. I'll pay you a whole dollar. (Hold up the dollar bill for emphasis.) Who would like to do it? Let's see; how about Robert? Robert, I choose you. So, would you stand here and hold this clock, please? That will show you the time you are to start. (Give him the clock face showing 8:00 o'clock.)

I don't know if one person can do it all, though. I'd like someone else to come about noon to help Robert. (Hold up second clock, choose someone, and give him the clock to hold.)

You know, we still might not get it all finished. I think I'd better ask one more, someone who could come about 4:00 o'clock in the afternoon. He will only have to work about one hour. (Choose another person, and give him the clock showing his starting time.)

Now let's see. If they all work until 5:00 o'clock, Robert will work eight hours . . . and Tim will work five hours . . . and Danny will work only one hour. (If you wish, you might develop this through questions, allowing the children to give the answers.) And now I'm going to pay them. Here is a dollar for Robert, and a dollar for Tim, and a dollar for Danny. I'm going to pay them all the same.

But somehow that doesn't seem fair, does it? Robert worked so much longer than the others. He might feel that I didn't treat him fairly at all. But, I gave him exactly what I promised him. It's just that I gave the others so much more than they deserved.

Do you know that Jesus told a story just like this? He wanted to say the same thing about the way God treats us. Tim and Danny didn't earn their dollars, it's true. I gave them more than they had coming. And that's the way God is. He doesn't give us what we deserve, or we wouldn't get anything, especially not life in heaven with him. God gives out of his love. We don't deserve that love, and we can never work hard enough to earn it. No matter how hard we try we just can't pretend that God owes us anything because we're his people. We're his people because he loves us, and sent Jesus to us. We don't even deserve to have our sins taken away. Jesus did that for the same reason . . . his love. And that's our good news! He is always giving us something we don't deserve . . . his love.

Soil for the Seed

SCRIPTURE

And when a great crowd came together and people from town after town came to him, he said in a parable: "A sower went out to sow his seed; and as he sowed, some fell along the path, and was trodden under foot, and the birds of the air devoured it. And some fell on the rock; and as it grew up, it withered away, because it had no moisture. And some fell among thorns; and the thorns grew with it and choked it. And some fell into good soil and grew, and yielded a hundredfold." As he said this, he called out, "He who has ears to hear, let him hear."

Luke 8:4-8   (Sexagesima Sunday)

PREPARATION

Prepare four small containers, each to hold a different kind of soil. (For the containers, cut-off milk cartons serve very well.) In one, pack some soil very firmly, tamping it until the surface is very hard. Fill the second with a small amount of soil and a larger amount of pebbles. Put some soil in third, but fill it with weeds. (Paper cut to look like weeds will be suitable if there are no weeds available at the season.) In the fourth carton, place some well-prepared soil.

Some of you have probably planted gardens, or have helped father and mother when they did. How many have? (Allow response.) So, I wonder if you can tell me which one of these boxes would make the best garden. (Show each one, and allow the children to comment.) It's this last one, isn't it? Look how well the soil is prepared for planting. Seed would grow well there, I am sure.

But let's look at the others, too, and try to figure out why they would not be so good. Look how hard-packed the soil is in this first one. Why, the seed wouldn't even get into the ground before birds would come along and eat it.

This next one isn't so good, either. There are so many rocks and pebbles the seed just couldn't get roots down very deep. And without deep roots, a plant dies quickly, doesn't it?

And this one is a problem, too. It looks like a garden for weeds instead of for good plants. We know that weeds will choke out good plants.

We were right before. The last box is the good soil. Our garden will grow in this one.

But really, we're not talking just about gardens and soil. We are really talking about people. We're talking about how we grow as the children of God. The seed is his word, and he wants us to be the right soil, hearing the word, growing in the way we listen to it and live with it. That is the good fruit he wants our gardens to produce.

We have to admit though, that we're not always such good soil. Sometimes we think we're too busy to hear the word of God at all. Then we're just like that packed-down soil, where the seed can't even start. Then sometimes it seems we have rocks in our heads, with so many other things to think about the word just gets started but then dies out. And sometimes we're so interested in other things, those things choke out the word, just like weeds in a garden. That's why Jesus told this story. He wanted to warn us these things do happen.

But he did something more than just warn us. He came to change us, and he still comes to change us. That's the good news we have in this story. Jesus came to make us good soil. And that means we can produce a garden of good fruit!

Love Is the Greatest

SCRIPTURE

So faith, hope, love abide, these three; but the greatest of these is love.

1 Corinthians 13:13 (Quinquagesima Sunday)

PREPARATION

Collect pictures of various activities of church life, such as people singing, praying, talking to each other, listening to a sermon, or placing an offering in the offering basket. Also add a few pictures of people at various other activities, such as work, study, play. From construction paper cut out a heart.

(An alternate possibility for the visual material is a set of simple line drawings, showing a music staff for the singing, folded hands for the praying, an open Bible for the word. Include the heart in this set of drawings too.

There is one reason we are here this morning, and I wonder if anyone knows what it is? (Allow responses.) Many of the things you said were just very close to what I was thinking about. My reason is that we are here because we are God's children. We became his children when we were baptized. We are his children because Jesus has taken away our sins. That's why we're here. Coming together to worship is something God's children do.

Let's look at these pictures to see some of the things God's people do. (Hold up first picture, and allow response. Follow with second picture, and so on, through the list of the "church" activities.) We do these things together, don't we? We tell God how much we love him in our songs; we tell him how much we need him in our prayers; we show him we want to do his will when we listen to his word. Those are things God's people do.

Now, here are some other things God's people do. (Show the pictures of the "non-church" activities.) The way we work shows we love God; the way we play shows it too. These are things God's people do, too.

It's funny, though, God said that the most important thing his children do is something we haven't seen yet . . . even though we said all the other things show it. It's this. (Hold up heart.) But what does that mean? (Allow response.) You're right! It's a heart, and it means love. And God said that's the greatest thing of all. We can sing together (hold up picture) but if we don't love God and each other, our songs are just a lot of noise to him. Or we can pray, but if we don't love each other, our prayers are just words. And so with this—or this— or this—. (Hold up pictures to illustrate the various activities.) This is the greatest, God says. (Hold up heart once more.)

And that's why Jesus came. He brought us this greatest gift of God, and he turns us around so that we can live in the greatest way with each other. He didn't come just to sing songs about God, although he and his disciples did sing some hymns. He came to share God's love. He didn't just pray to God about it, although he did that, too. He did something about it by loving people. For Jesus, love didn't mean just talking or listening about God's love, but acting it, showing it, and living with it. For Jesus doing love meant even going to the cross to die. That was the greatest thing his love could do.

And that's why love is the greatest for us, too. Jesus lives in us, and shows his love through us. He has taken our sins away, and has put his love in their place. And that makes everything different. Singing is a great way to praise God; praying is wonderful; listening is important. But do you know something—love is the greatest!

The Easy Way

SCRIPTURE

Then Jesus was led up by the Spirit into the wilderness to be tempted by the devil. And he fasted forty days and forty nights, and afterward he was hungry. And the tempter came and said to him, "If you are the Son of God, command these stones to become loaves of bread." But he answered "It is written,

'Man shall not live by bread alone, but by every word that proceeds from the mouth of God.' "

Then the devil took him to the holy city, and set him on the pinnacle of the temple, and said to him, "If you are the Son of God, throw yourself down; for it is written,

'He shall give his angels charge of you,'

and

'On their hands they will bear you up, lest you strike your foot against a stone.' "

Jesus said to him, "Again it is written, 'You shall not tempt the Lord your God.' " Again, the devil took him to a very high mountain, and showed him all the kingdoms of the world and the glory of them; and he said to him, "All these I will give you, if you will fall down and worship me." Then Jesus said to him, "Begone, Satan! for it is written,

'You shall worship the Lord your God and him only shall you serve.' "

Then the devil left him, and behold, angels came and ministered to him.

Matthew 4:1-11 (First Sunday in Lent)

PREPARATION

Prepare three newspapers with mock headlines as follows:

PASTOR TO JUMP FROM CHURCH!

PASTOR TO HEAL CRIPPLED MAN!

PASTOR TO RAISE DEAD MAN TOMORROW!

These newspapers can be prepared by pasting blank paper over the normal headlines, and lettering in the new copy, or preferably, by cutting the necessary letters from other newspaper headlines and pasting them in place. This latter method produces a more realistic appearance, but either way produces the same results.

Suppose last night everyone in Temple Terrace (substitute the name of your own city) had seen this headline. (Show first paper.) What does it say? (Have one of the children read it.) What do you think would have happened this morning? I think our parking lot would have been so crowded this morning the line of traffic waiting to get in would have been three blocks long. Or suppose people had seen this. (Show second paper.) Or suppose this had been the headline. (Show third paper.) Do you think there would have been an empty place in church today? No, I don't think so either. And do you know, if God would only give me the power to do those things, we could fill our church. Things would be so easy then.

And that's really the way we like things. We like to have the easy way. You know, if God would make everybody well, right now, it would be an easy thing for us to see his power. Or if he would only stop the war today, that would be an easy thing for us to see. It would really prove that he is God. Or if he would make certain that we never have any troubles or will never get sick or never have any accidents, we could believe in him very easily. And we'd like that. We like to take the easy way.

That's exactly what the devil wanted Jesus to do, too. He wanted Jesus to take the easy way. The devil was trying to trick Jesus, to make him think he could have his kingdom without suffering or dying for it, without going to the cross.

But Jesus didn't listen to the devil. He didn't take the easy way. He took the harder way, the way of loving people and helping them and even dying for them. And that's the way for us, too. It's not the easy way, but it's the way of Jesus. And that means it's the only way!

Called to Be Clean

SCRIPTURE

For God has not called us for uncleanness, but in holiness.
1 Thessalonians 4:7 (Second Sunday in Lent)

PREPARATION

The visual aids for this message are two paper dolls, one obviously a boy doll and one obviously a girl doll. They should have different hair styles, different clothes, and perhaps even hold something to represent different activities.

Do you see what I have in my hands this morning? That's right, I have two dolls. But notice something; they are different. I wonder if someone can tell me what the difference is? (Allow time for response.)

That's right, one is a boy doll and one is a girl doll. We all know that, don't we? But how did you tell them apart? (Allow children to answer, directing them to differences which they might not mention.)

But to tell the truth, I like both of these dolls. And if they were mine, I'd like either one as much as the other. And I wouldn't want this one to beat up on this one. (Show boy doll first and the girl, as you say that sentence.) And I wouldn't want this one to try to boss this one or pretend something to trick this one. (Reverse the order.) If these were my dolls, I'd want them to love each other, to care for each other, to help each other, and to make each other happy.

Now I see 12 of you like this. (Show girl doll, and give the number.) And I see 14 of you like this. (Show boy doll, and give that number.) We know that these dolls are different, and we know that you are different, too. We even know why we're different. We're different because God made us that way.

But God doesn't want us to use these differences against each other, either. If boys are stronger, that

43

doesn't mean they should beat up on girls. Or if girls are prettier, it doesn't mean they should use being pretty to trick the boys. Notice I just said *IF*. But the meaning is real. God doesn't want us to make fun of the differences, or anything like that, or to use them against each other. That would be spoiling something good that God has made. Actually he made us different so that we would want to love each other and care for each other and make each other happy.

That's why Jesus came for all of us. He knew that we would see the differences in each other. And he knew that sometimes we would try to use those differences in the wrong way. That would be sin. So he came to our world, to take away our sin. He puts his love and his caring and his making people happy in its place. That changes us.

It means that we can see ourselves and each other in a different way. We can say, "I'm a boy, and that's good." or "I'm a girl, and that's good, too!" Especially we can say, "I'm a child of God, and that's best of all!"

The Strong and the Stronger

SCRIPTURE

"But if it is by the finger of God that I cast out demons, then the kingdom of God has come upon you. When a strong man, fully armed, guards his own palace, his goods are in peace; but when one stronger than he assails him and overcomes him, he takes away his armor in which he trusted, and divides his spoil.

Luke 11:20-22 (Third Sunday in Lent)

PREPARATION

As the children come forward for this message, ask two of them to help you. You will need one very small boy and one larger one, obviously older, larger, and stronger than the first. (Try to choose children who will respond, so that you need not prompt their actions beforehand. The demonstration will be more meaningful if it is natural.)

This morning I need two boys to help me. Who will help? Let's see. (Make a show of choosing.) I would like Mark and Chuck to help me, if they will. Mark, will you come here, please? And Chuck, stand here, please.

Now, Chuck, I want you to take Mark's arm, just like this, and hold it very tightly, please. Don't let him get away, no matter how hard he pulls. Do you understand? All right, take his arm, then.

Now Mark, I want you to get away from Chuck. Pull! (Wait just a little, while Mark is obviously trying to pull away.) Come on, Mark, we're waiting. (Wait just a short time longer.) What's the matter, Mark? (Hopefully, he will answer, and you can direct his answer to the fact that Chuck is too strong, or too big, or some answer similar to those.) You mean Chuck is too strong for you, isn't he? I can understand that. He's older and bigger than you are. So let me help you. (Pull Chuck's hand away.) Now you're free, Mark. You're free because I'm even stronger than Chuck.

And Jesus told us that's exactly what life is like always.

45

He said that the devil is like a strong man who takes hold of us, and we can't get away. But then Jesus is the stronger one. Just as I took Chuck's hand away from Mark's, so Jesus took the devil's hold away from us. He set us free. That's really good news, isn't it? We're not held down by the devil any more. Jesus has taken away our sins, and has put the devil down. And that's what he does for us all the time, when he comes to us in his word or in the sacrament of communion. He is the stronger one. Really, he's the strongest! And he's on our side.

Wide-awake Worship

SCRIPTURE

Rejoice in the Lord, O you righteous! Praise befits the upright!

Praise the Lord with the lyre, make melody to him with the harp of ten strings!

Sing to him a new song, play skilfully on the strings, with loud shouts.

Psalm 33:1-3   (Fourth Sunday in Lent)

PREPARATION

You will need a child's doll which will close its eyes when lying down, and open them when upright.

I have a doll in my hands this morning who will help us share the word of God. But so that she can really help us, you'll have to notice something about her. I wonder if you can tell a difference when I hold her this way (hold the doll upright) or this way. (Hold her lying down.) Do you see the difference? This way her eyes are open (demonstrate) and this way they are closed. (Demonstrate.) Now she is awake (demonstrate) and now she is asleep. (Demonstrate again.)

But our little doll is really showing us something about how we worship God. God says worship is something to do! In one of the psalms he tells us to rejoice . . . and that's doing something. He tells us to praise him, and that's doing something too. He tells us even to sing and play on an instrument with loud shouts. Those are all things to do. And we have to be awake to do them. (Demonstrate with doll.)

But sometimes we're more like this. (Show doll lying down.) Oh, I don't mean that we go to sleep during worship, although sometimes even that happens. But when we just sit back and let others worship, it's like being asleep. When we let others sing or praise God or

47

pray, we're not doing much worshiping ourselves. We're just not wide-awake worshippers!

That's why we need our Lord Jesus all the time. He erases our sleepiness with his love; he wakes us up with his forgiveness. He sends his Spirit to us to open our eyes to his goodness. (Bring doll upright so that the eyes open.) Jesus didn't let anything get in the way of his love for us, and he takes away those things that get in the way of our worship. That's the good news God's people have, and the good news we can share in worship today! So why let others do it alone? (Hold doll flat.) Let's wake up and worship! (Hold upright again.)

With New Batteries

SCRIPTURE

. . . How much more shall the blood of Christ, who through the eternal Spirit offered himself without blemish to God, purify your consciences from dead works to serve the living God.

Hebrews 9:14 (Fifth Sunday in Lent)

PREPARATION

You will need a two-cell flashlight, in working condition except for the batteries, which should be dead. You will also need two new batteries with which to replace the dead ones. You will also need a cross.

I had some trouble this morning. I wanted to use my flashlight, but I found that it didn't work. The switch is good, and the bulb is all right, too. The case looks good. I wonder what's wrong with it. (Allow response from the children. Someone will say "The batteries.")

Let's see if it could be the batteries. (Open flashlight and take out the batteries.) They look good, but we'll just have to see what happens when I put these new batteries in. (Replace the batteries as you are talking, filling in with other statements as necessary about how you hope it works, etc.) Now, let's try it. And there we are. (Shine light on children.) A flashlight can't work with dead batteries, can it?

But our flashlight is a sort of story about God's people, too. We can't work with dead batteries, either. When people are afraid of God, or try to do all sorts of good things so that God has to love them, or try to keep a lot of rules so that they can go to heaven, they have old batteries. The Bible even calls those "dead works." We can't really serve God or even love each other unless someone gives us new power.

And that's what Jesus did. Just like I took out the dead batteries and put the new ones in, so he took out our "dead works" and put his love and his forgiveness in their place. That's the way he turns us on.

For me it was a simple thing to take off this cap and put new batteries in. But for Jesus there was more. For him, it meant this. (Show the cross.) But that's the way he makes us alive again, makes us people with new batteries. He makes us turned-on Christians.

A Different King

SCRIPTURE

Have this mind among yourselves, which you have in Christ Jesus, who, though he was in the form of God, did not count equality with God a thing to be grasped, but emptied himself, taking the form of a servant, being born in the likeness of men. And being found in human form he humbled himself and became obedient unto death, even death on a cross.

Philippians 2:5-8   (Palm Sunday)

PREPARATION

Prepare a set of very simple line drawings, showing a king's throne, a crown, a palace, a crown of thorns, and a cross.

What kind of person would use these things? (Show the throne, the palace, and the crown. You may wish to build it up by asking about the throne first, then suggesting you will give another hint, etc. In that case, hold the crown, the most easily identified, until last.) That's right, a king would use them. A throne and a palace and a crown are symbols for a king; they are signs of his great power.

When Jesus came into Jerusalem one day, a day called Palm Sunday, many people came out to meet him. They hoped he would be their king. Whether they would have given him this (show throne) or this (show palace) or this (show crown) we don't know. Perhaps they thought he would be so powerful he would take them anyway. But they became very unhappy when he didn't want them. He didn't want that kind of power; he didn't come to be that kind of king.

Instead, Jesus came for these. (Show crown of thorns and cross. Allow children to identify them, and to explain them.) He didn't come to rule over people; he came to serve them. His power was his love, and his throne was his cross. He was a different king.

And so he makes us different people, too. We like to

51

have power over others, to be kings over them if we can. We like to tell them what to do, and we like them to do the things we tell them. We like to be rulers and have others be our servants. But instead, Jesus gives us a new way . . . a way of serving others. He loves us so that we can love them; he forgives us, so that we can forgive each other. He came to be a friend, and so we can be friends with each other. That's the way his kingdom operates, because that's the kind of king he is . . . and that's the kind of people we can be. That's good news, because he's a good king!

It's Empty!

SCRIPTURE

But on the first day of the week, at early dawn, they went to the tomb, taking the spices which they had prepared. And they found the stone rolled away from the tomb, but when they went in they did not find the body. While they were perplexed about this, behold, two men stood by them in dazzling apparel; and as they were frightened and bowed their faces to the ground, the men said to them, "Why do you seek the living among the dead? Remember how he told you while he was still in Galilee, that the Son of man must be delivered into the hands of sinful men, and be crucified, and on the third day rise."

Luke 24:1-7 (Easter Sunday)

PREPARATION

The only visual aid necessary for this message is a plastic egg which can be opened. If the egg is decorated the visual effect will be improved.

Who can tell me what this is? That's right, it's an egg. Of course, it isn't a real one, but we can all see that. It's a plastic egg, and this morning we're going to pretend that it's an Easter egg.

No, let's pretend that it's something else, something entirely different. Let's pretend that it's a grave. And do you know what a grave is? (Allow response from children.) That's right, a grave is a place where we put a dead body. And maybe you remember that when Jesus died they put his body in a grave. They even put a stone in front of it to close it up.

So now let's pretend this is the grave where they put Jesus' body. We're going to open it, to see what's inside. Can you see? (Hold open parts of the egg toward the children.) What is inside? (Wait for response.) It is empty, isn't it! How about that! It is empty!

That's really the good news for Easter. Jesus died on Good Friday, and on Easter morning he came out of the grave. It couldn't hold him in. (Move egg halves together slowly, but then pull them apart rapidly.) Jesus was stronger than the grave; he was stronger even than death. He came alive again.

And that's good news for us, too. Someday we will die. We hope it will be a long, long time from now. After all, God has given us life to live and enjoy and hold on to. But when we do die, we won't have to be afraid. Jesus went into the grave and came out again. (Close egg and open it as dramatically as possible.) We will do the same thing.

And today you may even have a happier day if you remember this every time you look at one of your Easter eggs. Let them remind you that Jesus is alive, and you will be, too.

Without a Doubt

SCRIPTURE

Now Thomas, one of the twelve, called the Twin, was not with them when Jesus came. So the other disciples told him, "We have seen the Lord." But he said to them, "Unless I see in his hands the print of the nails, and place my hand in his side, I will not believe."

Eight days later, his disciples were again in the house, and Thomas was with them. The doors were shut, but Jesus came and stood among them, and said, "Peace be with you." Then he said to Thomas, "Put your finger here, and see my hands; and put out your hand, and place it in my side; do not be faithless, but believing." Thomas answered him, "My Lord and my God!" Jesus said to him, "Have you believed because you have seen me? Blessed are those who have not seen and yet believe."

John 20:24-29 (First Sunday after Easter)

PREPARATION

Cut eight pieces of heavy paper or light cardboard approximately four inches by eight inches each. With a heavy marker, prepare the cards as follows:

Mark a circle approximately three inches in diameter in the bottom half of the card. This circle will be the outline for the happy face, the neutral face, or the unhappy face which will be the lower part of the card. Mark the cards in the following sequence:

1. A happy face.
2. A neutral face, mouth a straight line rather than smiling. Above the face draw a large question mark.
3. A sad face, with a question mark made with a broken line rather than a solid one, but the same size as the question mark on picture two.
4. A sad face, with a very heavy question mark above it.
5. A sad face, with a question mark the same as in picture two.
6. A neutral face, with same size question mark as previous card.
7. A happy face, but with the same size question mark as cards five and six.
8. A happy face, with a bold cross replacing the question marks.

Note: As you read the message below, you may wish to condense parts of it into a phrase or two to fit on the back of each card. This will make for easier presentation, since it will aid in keeping the cards in order. The presentation is also more effective if card one is in front, but then card two is brought from the back of the pack, and so on through all the cards.)

(Hold the cards so that only the first one can be seen.)

This morning I'm going to tell you about a boy named Tommy. Here is his picture. He's a happy boy, isn't he. He has a smiling face.

But one day Tommy had a problem. It was a question about something in Sunday school, and it bothered him. (Show card two.) Oh, he wasn't really sad, but he wasn't happy, either. He was just troubled a little. So, he first did this. (Show card three.) He tried to put it out of his mind. He pretended he hadn't thought of the question at all. But that didn't make him any happier; instead it made him sadder than before. Then he tried something else. He decided to stay away from Sunday school. He thought: "Well, since I'm not sure about it, I'll just stay away until I decide." But that didn't help either. (Show card four.) Instead his question got bigger and bigger, and he got sadder and sadder.

So he told some of his friends about his feelings, and that didn't help much either. One of them said, "That's a silly question!" and another one said, "You can't believe that!" That didn't help Tommy at all. He was still like this. (Show card five.)

But the next week he decided what to do. He came back to Sunday school. He wasn't too sure of himself, but he told his teacher about his question. (Show card six.) He wasn't happy about it, but he wasn't quite so sad. At least he had shared it with someone who would listen. But then something happened. The teacher said "Tommy, that's a very good question! Let's see if we can find an answer!" That was good news for Tommy. (Show card seven.)

But the best news was yet to come. The teacher and Tommy and the class all talked about the question, and they found the answer in Jesus' love. Now look at Tommy, and see the difference. But just think, if he had hidden his question, or had stayed away, or had never asked it, he might still be sad.

That's Living

SCRIPTURE

The thief comes only to steal and kill and destroy; I came that they might have life, and have it abundantly. I am the good shepherd. The good shepherd lays down his life for the sheep.

John 10:10, 11   (Second Sunday after Easter)

PREPARATION

From a catalogue or newspaper, cut out pictures of the following items, or substitutes for them: golf clubs, sewing machine, motorcycle, and record player. Also find pictures of a Bible and a cross, or use real ones, if you prefer.

I think all of us have probably heard someone say: "That's really living!" We usually say it when things are going just the way we want them to, or when we get to do the things we really want to do, or when we have the things we really like to have.

A man who plays golf might say "That's really living!" if someone were to give him these. (Show golf clubs.) Or a woman might say it if she gets this. (Show sewing machine.) Maybe an older brother would say "That's really living!" if he had one of these. (Show motorcycle.) And I suppose a sister might say the same if she received one of these. (Show the record player.) Of course, we could show a lot more pictures, couldn't we? There are so many things we'd like to have. If we just had them all we could say "We're really living!"

But Jesus told us that we might be fooled with all those things. We could have all those things and not be really living at all. You see, someone could steal the golf clubs. (Fold up the picture and set it aside.) Or the sewing machine could stop working. (Repeat the action with this picture.) The motorcycle could be in an accident. (Crumple it.) Even the record player could be broken. (Crumple it also.) And if those are the things which make life worthwhile, we wouldn't have much left, would we?

That's why when Jesus said that he came to give us life, he meant it in a different way. Of course he meant us to enjoy all these other things when we have them, but he meant something more. For Jesus living meant having God's love. That's why he said that he came to give us real living; he came to bring us God's love in a very special way, and to bring us life in a special way too. Really living means knowing that God has forgiven our sin, and always does; that he cares about us, and always will. That's why living starts with these. (Show Bible and cross.)

This is the way life comes to us. And the good news is that no one can take them away from us, and they won't rust or get broken. We have God's love. That's living. No, that's *really* living!

Smile, God Loves You

SCRIPTURE

Make a joyful noise to God, all the earth; sing the glory of his name; give to him glorious praise!

Psalm 66:1-2   (Third Sunday after Easter)

PREPARATION

Prepare two very simple faces, using circles for the outline One is to be a smiling face, similar to the smile buttons now so popular. The other is to be a frowning face.

Sunday is a happy day, isn't it? Just think, no school today, no work today, more time to play, and even friends to see at Sunday school and church. It's a happy day.

Of course, there's another reason Sunday is a happy day, and a much better reason really. Sunday is a little celebration of Easter. When God's people come together on Sunday morning they remember that Jesus came out of the grave on a Sunday. He had won the fight with sin. He really gave us something to be happy about. Sunday is just a time to remind us of it all.

Maybe we can remind each other this morning. Look at this little fellow. (Show the sad face.) He's not very happy at all, is he? He's remembering all the bad things he has done . . . how he got angry with his brother, or how he told a lie to his mother, or even how he cheated in a test in school. It's easy to see why he's so sad. He's thinking about all those things.

But now, let's look at this other little guy. He was just like his brother at first, thinking about all the things he had done. But then he remembered all the wonderful things Jesus had done for him. That's why he's smiling! He's thinking about the love Jesus has for him, and the forgiveness Jesus gives him. Just think, all the bad things are taken away. He doesn't have to worry about them

59

any more. Jesus changed him from this (show sad face) to this (show happy face).

Sometimes we're just like this sad little fellow, though, and then even Sunday isn't so much fun for us. It's not a happy day if we remember our sins, but don't remember God's love.

So now let's help each other. Show me with your faces how you feel when you think of the bad things you have done. (Indicate sadness with your own expression.) That's called confession. But let's not stop there. Show me how you feel when you remember all the good things Jesus has done. (Wait for the smiles to appear.) That's better. That's called forgiveness, and it even feels better, doesn't it?

Now, show your parents how you feel about Jesus. (Wait just a short time.) Maybe that will help them feel happy, too.

Sing a Happy Song!

SCRIPTURE

O sing to the Lord a new song, for he has done marvellous things.

Psalm 98:1 (Fourth Sunday after Easter)

PREPARATION

On heavy paper or light cardboard draw a music staff with several notes. (This should be accurate musical notation, so if necessary, enlist the help of the organist or some music student to prepare this.) The notes should be the first notes of the children's song *Jesus Loves Me.*

On the reverse side of the paper, draw another music staff with notes also, but have this staff distorted, have the notes mis-shaped, and the lines irregular.

Also, enlist the help of someone from the congregation to lead the children in singing as a concluding response, if you are not comfortable doing it yourself.

This morning I want you to see a song. That's right, to see a song. Most of the time we sing a song or we hear a song, but first this morning we are going to see a song. Here it is. (Display the music.) That's a song most of you know. These are the notes for *Jesus Loves Me, This I Know.* And if all of us could read the music, we could look at this and sing it, and that would be fun.

It would be fun because it is a happy song. It tells us that Jesus loves us. It's the kind of song God's people can sing . . . songs about his love, songs about the wonderful things he does for us, happy songs, praising songs, thanking songs, just like this. (Hold up music again.)

But sometimes, things interrupt our happy songs. Our lives seem to be turned around, and we forget to sing our happy songs to God. We forget to thank him and to praise him. We get worried about things, or upset about other things. Our music is turned around. (Turn card around to show the distorted music.) I wouldn't even try to sing this one. Just look how mixed-up it is . . . just like we are sometimes.

That's why Jesus came to us. He saw that his people were often turned around and that their songs weren't as happy as they could be. So he came to turn us the right way again. (Turn card.) Instead of bad music, he gave us happy songs . . . the happy sounds of his love and his forgiveness to us. We're his people and we can sing our new songs to him again. Jesus loves us, and all the great things he has done for us tell us so!

Maybe we can show our fathers and mothers how a happy song sounds! Let's do! (Have the person you prompted begin singing *Jesus Loves Me*, preferably without accompaniment, since this will show the children's voices better.)

Something to Do

SCRIPTURE

But be doers of the word, and not hearers only, deceiving yourselves.

James 1:22 (Fifth Sunday after Easter)

PREPARATION

Using wrapping ribbon and gold seals of the type used on various church certificates, prepare two simulated medals. Construction paper can be used in place of the notary seals if they are unavailable.

With a heavy marking pen, mark one ribbon to read "I READ THE WHOLE BIBLE!" and mark the other to read "I MEMORIZED ONE HUNDRED SIX BIBLE PASSAGES."

This morning I want to tell you a story about a *very* religious person. Why, he was just about the most religious person you ever saw. He never missed Sunday school, and that's very good! And he never missed church, and that's very good too. He was so religious he even got medals for it. Here is one medal. Can anyone read it? Right! He won this medal for reading the whole Bible all the way through. Would you believe that he read the whole thing?

And here's his other medal. Let's see why he received this one. (Have someone read it.) That's right, too. He memorized one hundred six Bible passages. That's really something, isn't it. He was very religious!

But let me tell you something more. He went to Sunday school one morning and memorized the Bible verse that says "Love one another." Then he went to church, and he heard God's word about being kind and considerate and helpful to one another. But that afternoon when his little sister needed some help with her wagon, he became angry with her, and wouldn't help. When his father asked him to mow part of the lawn, he ran off to play with his friends. Even when his grandmother came to see him, he didn't come home; he wanted to play baseball. He read the word about loving; he even memorized a Bible passage about loving. But he didn't do it. He wasn't so religious after all, was he? The Bible tells us that real religion is not just hearing the word of God, but doing it as well.

That's the kind of religion Jesus brought to us. He knew that we would often be satisfied with just hearing instead of doing. So, he came to change us, to take away our sins of lazy, do-nothing religion. He forgives those, and sends his Spirit to us so that we can be a people who do his word.

Why, Jesus himself came to be a doer and not just a hearer. He didn't just talk about loving people; he loved them, and he still does. He didn't just talk about taking away our sins, or listen to others who talked about forgiveness. He did the taking away; he does the forgiving! And because he was a doer, we can be, too. You see, one of the things he does is that he lives in us, and he gives us religion to do.

Love Covers Us

SCRIPTURE

Above all, hold unfailing your love for one another, since love covers a multitude of sins.

1 Peter 4:8   (Sixth Sunday after Easter)

PREPARATION

On three separate pieces of paper, preferably at least five by eight inches or larger, draw stick figures, each holding a placard. On the one placard write the word SELFISH; label the second ANGRY; label the third, UNLOVING.

Cut three hearts from red construction paper, making them large enough to cover the placards. In the center of each heart mark a cross. On the back place a loop of masking tape or cellophane tape so that the heart can be fixed to the drawings, each to cover a placard.

This morning we're going to see our pictures. Would you like that? Of course you would. We always like to see our pictures. So here they are. Let's look at them. (Show the three pictures you have prepared.)

Actually, I was sort of fooling you. These aren't really our pictures in the usual way, the kind we might take with a camera. These are pictures which show what we're often like. Look at this one. It says that we are selfish, and many times we are. Or look at this. It tells us we're angry, and we are often that, too. And this one says that we are unloving, and we'd have to admit that too. That's why these are our pictures.

It's funny, we usually can't see ourselves that way, can we? It's much easier to see the sins other people have. In fact, that's really one of our biggest problems. We look for other people's sins. We criticize them, we look for their faults, we point them out, we even tell others. We just aren't very loving.

The Bible tells us that there is a better way to live, though. Do you see this? (Hold up a heart.) We know

65

that a heart stands for love, don't we? Now let's watch what happens to our pictures. (Place a heart over each placard, covering up the labels.) Do you see that? The heart covers up the word each person holds, just as love covers up their sins. That's just a way of showing that when we love someone we don't look for his sins; we don't try to criticize him; we don't search out his faults. Our love covers them up.

But do you see what is in the center of the heart? It's the cross of Jesus, and it's there because without it, that love couldn't happen. We would still be the way we were. But Jesus has covered our sins with his love. He has hidden them away behind his forgiveness, and that means we can be loving people again. His love covers us, and so our love can cover others, just like his. (Show hearts covering the placards once more.)

You're Different

SCRIPTURE

When the day of Pentecost had come, they were all together in one place. And suddenly a sound came from heaven like the rush of a mighty wind, and it filled all the house where they were sitting. And there appeared to them tongues as of fire, distributed and resting on each one of them. And they were all filled with the Holy Spirit and began to speak in other tongues, as the Spirit gave them utterance.

Acts 2:1-4 (Pentecost)

PREPARATION

The only materials needed are a rubber ball and a "Super-ball." Try to have them as identical as possible, although this is not absolutely necessary.

Do you see what I have in my hands? All of you know what they are, of course. I have a ball in each hand. Everyone knows that. Why, they even look alike. (Invite the children to suggest ways in which they are alike, size, shape, color, same material.) They really are much alike, aren't they? But do you know something? They're really quite different. Just watch.

First, I'll bounce this ball. (Bounce the rubber ball.) Now, I'll bounce this one. (Bounce the "Super-ball.") Do you see the difference? Let's do it again. See the difference now? The first one bounces only a short distance back to my hand; the other one bounces almost all the way back. I wonder why? (Allow the children to respond. You can be certain that someone will know immediately. The greater probability is that you will have had the answer before this time.)

That's right! This one is a "Super-ball." It looks like the other one, but it's really different. The manufacturer didn't make them the same. He put something else into this one.

Our word of God today tells us that something like

67

that has happened to us. We look like everybody else; we dress alike, talk alike, eat alike, everything. But God tells us that we are different. He made us different by sending his Holy Spirit to us. He makes us alive as Jesus' people; he gives us faith. We know that Jesus came to take away our sins, simply because the Spirit gives us that faith. That makes us different.

We said before the people who make these balls made this one a "Super-ball." We can't say the Spirit makes us super-people, but we can say he makes us God's people. He did it when we were baptized; he does it now when we hear his word, or when we take communion. Super-people, no; but God's people, yes. And there's something super about that, anyway!

Giving God Advice

SCRIPTURE

O the depth of the riches and wisdom and knowledge of God! How unsearchable are his judgments and how inscrutable his ways!

"For who has known the mind of the Lord, or who has been his counselor?"

Romans 11:33-34   (Trinity Sunday)

PREPARATION

With a heavy marking pen, prepare three cards as follows:

1. C_2H_5OH

2. incommensurability

3. an outline map of your state, with your own town as a dot on it.

This morning we're going to take a short intelligence test. You know what those are. The teacher gives you a question sheet, and you have to give the answers. The only difference is that I have some question cards instead. Is everybody ready?

Here is the first one. Tell me what it is! Hold up your hand if you know! Anyone? Well, then I'll have to tell you; it's a chemical formula, the one for alcohol. I wonder if anyone can tell me if I wrote it correctly. No, I don't suppose we can even do that.

So let's go on to part two. This is a spelling test. Please look at this word and tell me if I have spelled it correctly. Who knows? Perhaps you haven't learned that word yet.

So let's go to part three of our test. What is this? (Some of the children will probably be able to tell you.) Good. But can you tell me if our town is in exactly the right place? That makes it harder, doesn't it?

This test shows us that we don't know everything. It would be foolish to pretend that we did. Unless you know something about chemistry, you would be foolish to correct my card; unless you know how to spell that big word, you would be foolish to tell me it's wrong. Even unless you know our state map, you would be foolish to correct mine.

And that's true in other ways, too, and especially with God. We would like to correct the way he does things. We get sick and complain "Why does it have to happen to me?" We lose a ballgame and we wonder why God seems to let us lose all the time. Or we ask why God doesn't heal all the sick people of the world, or end all the wars in the world, and so on. We're like Adam and Eve, the first people. They wanted to be like God. They wanted to take his place. That was their sin, and it is ours, too.

But we have some good news about it all. When we want to tell God just what to do, when we want to take his place, that is sin, of course. But God knew exactly what he wanted to do about that. Instead of letting us take his place, he sent his son to take ours. Jesus went to the cross to die for us, so that all complaining and trying to give God advice could be forgiven. Now we can live with his forgiveness, instead of offering him our advice. We can be happy that God has the answers.

Something to Live For

SCRIPTURE

". . . And he said, 'Then I beg you, father, to send him to my father's house, for I have five brothers, so that he may warn them, lest they also come into this place of torment.' But Abraham said, 'They have Moses and the prophets; let them hear them.' And he said, 'No, father Abraham; but if some one goes to them from the dead, they will repent.' He said to him, 'If they do not hear Moses and the prophets, neither will they be convinced if someone should rise from the dead.'"

Luke 16:27-31 (First Sunday after Trinity)

PREPARATION

In a small box, possibly of shoe-box size, place a number of items of interest to children, or pictures of these items. Included might be a toy car, a picture of a house, a baseball, a small doll, a dollar bill, a simulated report card with all A's on it, and a picture of Jesus Christ.

I have a box full of surprises this morning, and I think you will like all the things I have in my box. Let's see. Here is something most of you will like. (Show the toy car.) And your fathers and mothers would like one, too, I suppose, only a real one. People will work very hard to earn enough money to buy one. Or look at this. (Show picture of a house.) We all like nice houses, and we'll work hard to get them, and work hard to keep them looking right.

Here are some other things. (Show baseball and doll.) And look at this; we all like money. We work hard to earn it, and we enjoy spending it. And here is something else . . . a straight A report card. We'd all like that, wouldn't we? Actually, we like everything our box contained.

But do you know that we could have our whole box filled with these good things, but someday they would all disappear, and we would have nothing left. So, maybe we'd better see if there is something else in our box.

71

(Hold out picture of Christ.) Yes, there is! And do you see who it is? Right! It's Jesus! And he's in our box for a very special reason. He wants to be there . . . not in a box, of course, but in our lives. And when everything else is gone, he will still be there.

That really gives us something better to live for, right now. It means we can enjoy all these other things. (Point to items from box.) We can even enjoy them more because he gave them to us. But we don't have to let them take his place. He came to take his place with us, and he will never be gone. That's good news! We not only have something to live for, we have someone to live with.

So Much to Do

SCRIPTURE

But he said to him, "A man once gave a great banquet, and invited many; and at the time for the banquet he sent his servant to say to those who had been invited, 'Come, for all is now ready.' But they all alike began to make excuses. The first said to him, 'I have bought a field, and I must go out and see it; I pray you, have me excused.' And another said, 'I have bought five yoke of oxen, and I go to examine them; I pray you, have me excused.' And another said, 'I have married a wife, and therefore I cannot come.' "

Luke 14:16-20   (Second Sunday after Trinity)

PREPARATION

The visual aids for this message are a filled-out invitation to a birthday party, three letters (preferably sealed, typewritten for the children to read), a Bible, and three other letters of supposed response to the Bible. (The dramatic action will be improved if all the letters are sealed, since opening them provides more impact.)

This morning we need some helpers again, but even before we need the helpers, let me tell you about something. I decided to have a birthday party, and I sent out invitations just like this one. It says "Please come to my birthday party on Saturday, _____ (Give date.) I sent these invitations a week ago, because I wanted everyone to know in plenty of time.

And now I have three letters from people who answered my invitation. I wonder if someone would help me read them. (Pick children who will be able to read easily.)

Dear Pastor:

I'm sorry I can't come to your birthday party, but I am going to get a new car that day, so I won't be able to come.

Oh, that's too bad. Well, let's hear the next one. (Have second child read.)

Dear Pastor:

I received your invitation to a party, but I won't be able to come, since I might go away that day.

Now I don't feel quite as happy as I did. But let's hear the last one. (Have third child read.)

Dear Pastor:

I am sorry that I can't come to your party, but my favorite TV program is on then, and I can't miss it.

That makes me feel sad. But of course, we were just pretending. Still it makes me feel sad that people will find other things to do instead of coming to my party.

But now let's talk about something else. We have a party right here. We're celebrating how much God loves us; we're celebrating that Jesus is coming to us right now in his word and his sacrament. We could even call his word an invitation. (Show Bible.) But let's hear some of these answers. (Open letters one by one to read them.)

Dear Jesus,

I'm sorry I can't come to your party, but Sunday is the only day I can sleep in.

or

Dear Jesus,

I won't be able to come to your party Sunday morning because that's the only day our family can have a picnic.

or

Dear Jesus,

I'll have to miss your party because we have company coming Sunday noon, and Mother has to make a big dinner and I have to clean my room.

Those letters don't sound too good, do they? In fact, they sound like excuses people make when they let other things get in the way of Jesus' celebration.

But there is good news, even for excuse-making people. Jesus continues to give his party. He still invites us with his word, and he still shows his love for us in the sacraments. He didn't make any excuses for himself. He doesn't let anything get in the way of his love for us and his forgiveness to us. That's why we can be happy people, and even ask Jesus for more strength to answer every invitation. He never has too much to do to remember us!

74

Lost: One Coin

SCRIPTURE

"Or, what woman, having ten silver coins, if she loses one coin, does not light a lamp and sweep the house and seek diligently until she finds it? And when she has found it, she calls together her friends and neighbors, saying, 'Rejoice with me, for I have found the coin which I had lost.' Even so, I tell you, there is joy before the angels of God over one sinner who repents."

Luke 15:8-10   (Third Sunday after Trinity)

PREPARATION

Before the service begins, place one coin where it will be hidden to the casual eye, but yet will be noticed when the children are directed to look for it. Have nine other coins available for use in the presentation.

Today we want to talk about how important we are to Jesus, and we're even going to tell a story which he told when he was explaining it to people years ago. He said it's like a person who has ten coins, just like I have here. (Hold out the coins, asking the children to count them. When they count only nine, be properly surprised, and eventually upset.) We just can't go on until we find that other coin. It must be here someplace. (Direct the children to look for it, and if it is not found quickly, help someone find it.) Good! Now we can go on. I thought for a minute we would have to sweep the whole building.

And that's exactly what Jesus said life in his kingdom is like. When one coin is missing, a person stops everything to find it. It is that important! And Jesus tells us that we are that important to him, too.

That's something to remember! Sometime when we feel blue, and feel that no one likes us, or feel that we're not very important, it's time to remember that we are! Jesus even came to earth to look for us, because we were lost. Our sins had taken us away from him, and he had to come to find us, and to bring us back again. We were happy when we found our lost penny, and Jesus tells us that even the angels are happy when he finds his lost people.

Just think! Angels are happy when Jesus finds us. We are important!

Keeping Our Eyes Closed

SCRIPTURE

And when he drew near and saw the city he wept over it, saying, "Would that even today you knew the things that make for peace! But now they are hid from your eyes."

Luke 19:41, 42 (Fourth Sunday after Trinity)

PREPARATION

Since this is a message involving the children in acting, there will be no materials to prepare. The only object necessary is a cross, large enough for all to see.

This morning I want to tell you a story about a little boy named Tommy. He looked just like any other boy, but he had one very different habit. Every time something was wrong, he would close his eyes, just like this. (Shut your own eyes tightly.) He did that for a reason. When he closed his eyes, he couldn't see that anything was wrong. Then Tommy could pretend that everything was all right.

Maybe all of you can pretend that you are like Tommy this morning, and whenever I mention that something is wrong, you might shut your eyes just as tightly as you imagine Tommy did. Let's even practice it once. (Allow time for all to shut their eyes tightly.) Now for the story.

One day at school, Tommy pushed his friend Timmy so hard that Timmy fell down and hurt his knee. When the teacher told Tommy that he was wrong, guess what Tommy did . . . or better yet, show me what he did! That's right; he closed his eyes. He didn't want to see it.

That afternoon when Tommy's friend Johnny told him "Tommy, that's not the right way to hold the bat, hold it like this." Tommy did the same thing. Can you show me again? And that evening, when his mother said "Tommy, just look at the mess in your room." Tommy

77

didn't look at all. Show me what he did! Right again! He closed his eyes. He didn't want to see that anything was wrong.

Now those are only little stories, but they are almost true for every one of us. We are so much like Tommy. We don't like to see anything wrong in things we do. Someone tells us that it is wrong to be selfish, or that we're not supposed to leave a mess in our room . . . or that someone needs help from us, or that we hurt someone's feelings, what do we do? That's right! All too often we close our eyes, and pretend that we don't see.

So, we really need something to open our eyes, don't we? And do you know, I have that right here. (Show the cross.) It sounds funny to say that the cross opens our eyes, but it does. Let's think about it.

You know that Jesus came to help people and to heal them. He opens our eyes so that we can see ourselves as we really are. But the difference is that when we see the cross too, we see God's love for us, even the way we are . . . and we see Jesus' forgiveness for the way we are. And when Jesus gives us the power to open our eyes, he also gives us the strength to live in a different way. We won't even have to close our eyes. He can keep them open with his love!

Tearing Up Your Love

SCRIPTURE

Finally, all of you, have unity of spirit, sympathy, love of the brethren, a tender heart and a humble mind. Do not return evil for evil or reviling for reviling; but on the contrary bless, for to this you have been called, that you may obtain a blessing.

1 Peter 3:8-9   (Fifth Sunday after Trinity)

PREPARATION

Cut two identical hearts from large pieces of heavy paper Use one at the beginning of the message; reserve the other for the conclusion.

We've all seen this shape many times. (Hold up one of the hearts.) We even know what it stands for, don't we? (Allow time for response. There will probably be answers of "Valentines," "hearts," and so forth. Let these be offered. It will be easy to go from them to the answer you want, which is "love.") That's right, a heart like this means love. And since we're God's people, we can look at it and be reminded of God's love to us. We can remember too that God's people are to share that love with everyone.

Wouldn't that be wonderful if we did share God's love like that? It's sad, but we don't. We get angry with each other. (Tear off a little part of the heart.) Sometimes we actually want to hurt each other. (Tear off more of the heart.) When someone does something to us, we like to get even. (Tear off more.) Or when someone says something bad about us, we say bad things about them. (Tear off the last parts, then tear up the remaining bit.) But look at our heart, our love. It's all gone. Our sins have torn it up. It's almost like Humpty Dumpty, and you remember that all the king's horses and all the king's men couldn't put him together again.

79

But maybe that's because Humpty Dumpty didn't have the kind of king we have. Our king is Jesus, and he doesn't just put our hearts back together again, he does something better! He gives us new ones.

The Bible tells us that we are to have tender hearts for each other. That's the kind of heart Jesus has for us. His love is so great that he even came to be one of us. He let people become angry with him, say bad things about him, and even make him suffer and die. But still he loved everyone, and he still does. He did everything so that we can have new hearts for him and for each other. (Hold up the new heart.) He gave them to us when we were baptized. He still gives us new hearts, every time we hear his word forgiving us, or every time we receive his body and blood in communion. He is picking up the pieces of our torn hearts, and giving us new ones in their place. Best of all, since he's with us, we don't have to tear up our hearts or hold back our love. We have tender hearts, because Jesus is living in them.

Two Directions

SCRIPTURE

"You have heard that it was said to the men of old, 'You shall not kill; and whoever kills shall be liable to judgment.' But I say to you that every one who is angry with his brother shall be liable to judgment; whoever insults his brother shall be liable to the council, and whoever says, 'You fool!' shall be liable to the hell of fire. So if you are offering your gift at the altar, and there remember that your brother has something against you, leave your gift there before the altar and go; first be reconciled to your brother, and then come and offer your gift. . . ."

Matthew 5:21-24 (Sixth Sunday after Trinity)

PREPARATION

For the visual aid for this message, cut two strips of heavy paper or light cardboard approximately two inches wide. Make one strip ten inches long, the other six inches long. On the longer one, print the word GOD at the top, and the word ME at the bottom. On the other strip, print the word BROTHER lengthwise on one end, and the word ME lengthwise on the other. Make a loop of masking tape or cellophane tape on the back of the shorter strip, so that you can attach it to the longer one to make a cross.

This morning we're going to talk about what it means to be a child of God. Maybe I can show you something to help you understand it.

You see, being a child of God for many people means this. (Show the longer strip.) It means that God loves me and I love God. It's a sort of vertical thing (make appropriate motion on the strip of paper) between God and me. And for many people, that's really all it is.

But others say, "Oh no, being a child of God means that I love my brothers." (Show shorter strip.) It means that I will be friendly and helpful and loving. It's a sort of horizontal thing. (Again, make the appropriate motion with your hands.) And for many people, that's all it is.

And do you know that both are partly right, but both are partly wrong. Being a child of God is something more than just either one alone. It's like this. (Show longer strip.) God loves me, and I love God. And it's like this. (Show shorter strip.) I love my brother, and I hope he loves me. That means both directions for the children of God. We love God and we love each other. (Put the two strips together.) Now let's see what we have. That's right; we have a cross. And it shows the love Jesus brought us . . . God's love as it reaches us (make vertical motion) and God's love as it reaches through us. (Make horizontal motion.) That's the sign of love, and it's the sign of the cross.

They Don't Mix

SCRIPTURE

I am speaking in human terms, because of your natural limitation. For just as you once yielded your members to impurity and to greater and greater iniquity, so now yield your members to righteousness for sanctification.

Romans 6:19 (Seventh Sunday after Trinity)

PREPARATION

In separate test tubes place equal amounts of water and cooking oil. (Note: Cap them tightly, and be certain to cap them during the message also.)

You can see that I have two test tubes in my hands this morning. (Display them.) In one I have water, and in the other I have oil. Now I'm going to pour them together. (Do so.) I'll put a cap on the test tube, and then I'd like someone to shake it very well and mix it up for me. (Choose a volunteer, and allow him enough time to shake the test tube.)

May I have it now? Let's all look at it, to see how our oil and water look when they're mixed up. (Hold it up to be seen.)

Oh, oh! We didn't get them mixed up yet, did we? Bobby, perhaps you didn't shake them hard enough. Would you like to try again? (Allow him more time.)

Now let's see. Look at that; they're still not mixed up. Maybe I should try it myself, since I'm a lot bigger than Bobby. (Shake the test tube vigorously, obviously harder than Bobby was able to.) There! If anything will do it, that will. Let's see if they're mixed up now. (Display the test tube.) Look at that! They still aren't mixed up. Well, since they won't mix, we'll just have to separate them again. (Pour the oil off into its own test tube.) I guess we've had a good chemistry lesson, though. Oil and water won't mix.

But we don't want to talk only about chemistry. We're really talking about something that happens in our lives, and about God telling us that good and bad don't mix, either. God has made us his children, and that means that bad thoughts or bad words or bad actions shouldn't get mixed up in our lives. They are like oil and water, and the thing to do is to separate the bad and keep it out.

That's exactly what God's Son did for us; he really did separate the bad from the good. When we have his forgiveness, it's like pouring out the oil, and leaving nothing but the good fresh water again. Maybe that's even why he said he gave people the water of life. It's not mixed in with anything bad. Oil and water don't mix. (Show test tubes again.) Neither do good and bad.

The Right Fruit

SCRIPTURE

"Beware of false prophets, who come to you in sheep's clothing, but inwardly are ravenous wolves. You will know them by their fruits. Are grapes gathered from thorns, or figs from thistles? So, every sound tree bears good fruit, but the bad tree bears evil fruit. A sound tree cannot bear evil fruit, nor can a bad tree bear good fruit. Every tree that does not bear good fruit is cut down and thrown into the fire. Thus you will know them by their fruits."

Matthew 7:15-20   (Eighth Sunday after Trinity)

PREPARATION

There are two possibilities for presenting this message. For the one, the visual aids will be two pieces of the same kind of fruit, with one a good piece of fruit, and the other a spoiled one.

The other approach is to use several different kinds of fruit, such as an apple, an orange, a banana, or others.

How much do we know about fruit and fruit trees? Let's name these things I have here. (Show the pieces of fruit, and allow the children time enough to name each one.) That was simple, wasn't it?

Now let's see if we know the trees these come from. (Show the pieces of fruit again, and have children identify each tree.)

(If you use the good and the rotten fruit, you might begin by asking "Which one of these would you rather have in your lunch at school tomorrow? Why? That's right; this is a good piece of fruit, and this is a rotten one." Then allow a short discussion of what a farmer would do if he found only rotten fruit on his trees. Talk about his disappointment, and how he would want his trees to produce good fruit.)

Now, let's suppose that a man owned an orchard, and he planted a lot of apple trees. When he went to get the fruit, he found oranges growing. (Or he found that the fruit was rotten.) He would say there was something wrong, wouldn't he? Or if he wanted bananas and got grapes, or something like that. He would certainly say there was something wrong with the trees, and he would try to make things right.

And Jesus said that's the way it is in his kingdom, too. He has told people to plant the word of God, so that we hear it and grow up with it. God's word is like the tree, and those who teach it and share it are those who plant it. The fruit comes when we learn to love God more and more, and to love each other more and more. Then the tree is bearing good fruit, the kind God expects. But if we stop loving God, or stop loving each other, then something is wrong. We're getting the wrong kind of fruit. (Show fruit again.)

So Jesus told his people to be certain the right fruit is growing. He came to plant himself in our lives, so that with his love and his forgiveness, we could be the right fruit. When our teachers and our pastors and our parents help us share his love and that forgiveness, then we are. That's the way his kingdom is to be. We have a good tree, and we can be good fruit!

What's in the Middle?

SCRIPTURE

"No servant can serve two masters; for either he will hate the one and love the other, or he will be devoted to the one and despise the other. You cannot serve God and mammon."

Luke 16:13   (Ninth Sunday after Trinity)

PREPARATION

Prepare the illustrations for this message either by drawing identical items on two sheets of paper, or by cutting pictures of the items from catalogues or newspapers, and pasting them on the two papers. With one exception, the sheets should be identical. Both should have all the items listed in the message, but on one the cross should be small and in the corner of the page, while on the other, it should be large and in the center.

We're going to look at two pictures this morning, pictures which are almost alike, but not quite. First let's look at this one. What do you see? (Allow the children to respond, naming the items or pointing to them as they do . . . a bicycle, a wagon, a TV set, a pair of roller skates, a doll, a microscope, a billfold, etc.) But notice, all of these things are on the picture, but there is something else, too. There is the cross of Jesus. So we've got just about everything, don't we?

Now let's look at this picture. It's almost the very same. The same things are there. (Point to them, and perhaps have children name them.) But there is a real difference. (Allow some time for the children to discover it, if they can. It may be necessary to lead them to it.) Let's look at them together. Now we can really see the difference. On this one the cross is right in the middle, but on this one it's pushed off into the corner.

It's too bad, but that actually happens with us. Jesus does get pushed into the corner. It happens when a confirmation student decides to watch TV and doesn't have his lesson done. It happens when someone decides to ride a bike all morning instead of going to Sunday school. It happens when these things become more important to us than Jesus is. Then they are in the middle, and he's in the corner. (Show the picture to illustrate.) That's bad news.

But we have good news to share this morning to take care of that bad news. The good news is that Jesus didn't stay pushed off in the corner. He came right into the middle of life, to be born a person just like every one of us. He lived and he died to take away even our sins of pushing him into the corner. He comes into the middle of life now in his word and his sacrament. Every time we hear his word, every time we share his forgiveness, every time we remember our baptism, every time we receive him in communion, Jesus is coming back into the center. He's there, right where he belongs!

Don't Blow Away

SCRIPTURE

Now concerning spiritual gifts, brethren, I do not want you to be uniformed. You know that when you were heathen, you were led astray to dumb idols, however you may have been moved. Therefore I want you to understand that no one speaking by the Spirit of God ever says "Jesus be cursed!" and no one can say "Jesus is Lord" except by the Holy Spirit.

1 Corinthians 12:1-3   (Tenth Sunday after Trinity)

PREPARATION

Cut a weathervane from a piece of heavy cardboard, and fasten it with a pin to the top of a pencil. Allow the vane to rotate freely when you blow it. (If you prefer, you can construct a weathervane from some children's construction sets, Tinkertoys, etc.)

It will be necessary to practice beforehand, for the experience in how hard to blow the vane. It may also be necessary to control the weathervane through moving the pencil.

Does anybody know what this is? (Wait for an answer; you may hear that it is an arrow, a dart, etc., before someone answers that it is a weathervane.) Now, can anyone tell me what this does? (Again, wait for the answer, knowing that you may even have to supply it yourself.) Do you see how it works? It tells us which way the wind is blowing. It points in the right direction.

God tells us that we're something like this weathervane. We point in a certain direction, too. We point to Jesus, and we say that he is our Lord. That's because we are his people. He came to earth to take our sins away, and his spirit is working in us to point us in the right way. (Blow the arrow so that it points to the cross in the chancel, if you have one . . . or to the altar, or to the Bible.) Just like this arrow points to the cross, so we point to Jesus.

But sometimes we get our directions turned around. (Blow the weathervane so that it spins.) It's just like this. We're pointed right, but then we get angry and forget Jesus. (Turn arrow away from cross.) Or, we're playing with a friend and our selfishness shows up. (Turn arrow again.) Or even when mother asks us to do something for her, we pout and fuss about doing it. (Turn arrow again.) Our directions get turned, and we don't point to Jesus then. We're turned around, or as our Bible word tells us, we are led astray.

Jesus came to turn us in the right direction. With his forgiveness he spins us around so that we point back to him. (Turn arrow back to the cross.) Every time we share his words, he is turning us back; every time we share him in communion, he turns us around again. He sends us his spirit, to point us back to the cross. (Turn arrow again.) We don't have to point in any other direction, and we don't have to spin around wondering which way to point. He won't let us blow away!

Lord, I'm Great!

SCRIPTURE

He also told this parable to some who trusted in themselves that they were righteous and despised others: "Two men went up into the temple to pray, one a Pharisee and the other a tax collector. The Pharisee stood and prayed thus with himself, 'God, I thank thee that I am not like other men, extortioners, unjust, adulterers, or even like this tax collector. I fast twice a week, I give tithes of all that I get.' But the tax collector, standing far off, would not even lift up his eyes to heaven, but beat his breast, saying, 'God, be merciful to me, a sinner!' I tell you, this man went down to his house justified rather than the other; for every one who exalts himself will be humbled, but he who humbles himself will be exalted."

Luke 18:9-14   (Eleventh Sunday after Trinity)

PREPARATION

Collect pictures showing people in various church activities. One might be a pastor, another a choir member, another several people in a committee meeting. (Church supply catalogues or church periodicals are excellent sources.) You will also need a light cardboard flash card, with the word PRIDE on one side, HUMILITY on the other.

We all like to be important, don't we? Even in church, we like to be important. But I wonder who is the most important. Let's look at some pictures of important people.

(Show picture of a pastor.) Now here's an important person. He might want to say "I thank you Lord that I am so important. If it weren't for me, the service just couldn't go on. I'm certainly glad that God made me so important."

Or look at this picture. (Show choir member.) She could say "I'm glad I'm so important. If it weren't for me, we wouldn't have such fine music in the church. I'm glad my voice is so much better than others. I'm important."

Or look at these men. (Show the committee meeting.)

Or look at these people. (Show people worshiping.) They might say "We're glad we're so important. We never miss a meeting or a church service. We give a lot of our time and even our money. We're important!"

Those things are easy for us to say, because we do like to be important. Sometimes we even think that God must like us better than he likes others. But that's just a sign we're mixed up by this sin. (Hold up card saying PRIDE.) Pride is the sin of feeling important when we really don't have any reason to, or really shouldn't.

But Jesus came to take away our sins of pride. You know, Jesus might have been very proud. But he set that aside to come to earth as a little baby, and when he grew up and went around his country teaching and healing and helping people, he still would not be proud. He wasn't even too proud to die for us to take our sins of pride away.

That's the good news we have today. He turns us around. (Turn card around, showing word HUMBLE.) Here is the opposite of being proud; it's being humble. That means knowing that we really aren't so much, after all. It means knowing we're just like everybody else. We're sinners. But we have Jesus! And that's really great, because he is!

Love or Law

SCRIPTURE

Such is the confidence that we have through Christ toward God. Not that we are sufficient of ourselves to claim anything as coming from us; our sufficiency is from God, who has qualified us to be ministers of a new covenant, not in a written code but in the Spirit; for the written code kills, but the Spirit gives life.

2 Corinthians 3:4-6   (Twelfth Sunday after Trinity)

PREPARATION

Make two folders, meant to represent books. Letter them as identically as possible on the outside, with the title *Being God's People.* Inside the first book print the following:

_____ I try to live perfectly always.

_____ I try to listen to God's Word perfectly.

_____ I try to keep all his commandments perfectly.

Inside the second book, put the line "I am a sinner!" at the top; make a large cross in the center, preferably in some bright color. At the bottom write in bold letters "I am forgiven!"

Since we are God's people, I thought it would be nice to have a little book telling us what it's like to be God's people. So I prepared this little book. Can someone read the title for me? (Allow it to be read, repeating if necessary for the adults in the congregation.)

Very good! Now let's open it and see what it says. Oh, it says that if I'm going to be one of God's people I have to try to live perfectly always . . . or listen to His Word perfectly . . . or keep all his commandments perfectly. (You may increase interest in this part of the presentation by having the children read.) Oh, that's bad news! I don't know if I've done all that. I'm not sure I can check this one . . . or this one . . . or even this one. I'm in trouble.

Perhaps we should look at this other book first, though. Let's see what it says. (Have one of the children read the title; then open it, and have them read the top line, and then the bottom. Call attention to the cross.)

Now that makes me feel much better. And really, that's the way Jesus talks about us as his people. It's not because we try to do all things (hold up first book) but because he has done this. (Hold up second book.)

But you know, it makes me feel so great to know I'm forgiven, that my love for Jesus grows and grows . . . and then something funny happens. I do try to do these things. (Show first book.) But it's different to do them because Jesus loves me. You see, we've got to keep our books straight; first comes this one. (Show the second book, pointing to the cross and to the words "I am forgiven!")

Am I Your Neighbor?

SCRIPTURE

But he, desiring to justify himself, said to Jesus, "And who is my neighbor?" Jesus replied, "A man was going down from Jerusalem to Jericho, and he fell among robbers, who stripped him and beat him, and departed, leaving him half-dead. Now by chance a priest was going down that road; and when he saw him he passed by on the other side. So likewise a Levite, when he came to the place and saw him, passed by on the other side. But a Samaritan, as he journeyed, came to where he was; and when he saw him, he had compassion, and went to him and bound up his wounds, pouring on oil and wine; then he set him on his own beast and brought him to an inn, and took care of him. And the next day he took out two denarii and gave them to the innkeeper, saying, 'Take care of him; and whatever more you spend, I will repay you when I come back.' Which of these three, do you think, proved neighbor to the man who fell among the robbers?" He said, "The one who showed mercy on him." And Jesus said to him, "Go and do likewise."

Luke 10:29-37   (Thirteenth Sunday after Trinity)

PREPARATION

For this message, you will need the help of a man from the congregation if this is presented when adults are present. Otherwise, you will have to enlist one of the older children.

I don't know how much we can talk this morning, because I have a headache. I was going to stop at the store to get some aspirins, but I discovered I left all my money at home. I'll just have to keep my headache, won't I?

But I have an idea. Mr. Smith is sitting in the front row. Maybe he can help me.

Mr. Smith, do you love me? (Have him prepared to stand up, answering, "Of course I do!")

Mr. Smith, I need some aspirins, and I forgot my money. Would you buy some for me, please?

(Mr. Smith should delay his answer for just a very short time, then say, "Well, I would like to, but I have just enough money to buy a paper and a magazine I want to get. I'm sorry, but if I get aspirins for you, I won't have enough money.")

(Wait just a short time, and then explain to the children that you had arranged this with Mr. Smith. Then ask them to listen as you ask him again.)

Mr. Smith, do you love me? (Follow the procedure as before, but this time, when you ask for the aspirins, Mr. Smith agrees immediately.)

Now, did you see the difference? The first time he said he loved me, but he had things he wanted for himself. He couldn't really share his money with me. The second time he forgot himself to do something for me. Which time was he my neighbor?

That's right! And that's exactly what Jesus said a neighbor is. A neighbor is someone who needs help, and we are neighbors when we give that help.

And Jesus said that's the way his people can live. They can be neighbors to each other, because he came to be a neighbor to us. He came to show his love to us, and to help us with the biggest problem of them all, our sin. But that's our good news today; Jesus takes away our selfishness and puts his love in its place. He is our loving neighbor, and he lives in us, so that we can be neighbors, too!

Our Two Faces

SCRIPTURE

Now the works of the flesh are plain: immorality, impurity, licentiousness, idolatry, sorcery, enmity, strife, jealousy, anger, selfishness, dissension, party spirit, envy, drunkenness, carousing, and the like. I warn you, as I warned you before, that those who do such things shall not inherit the kingdom of God. But the fruit of the Spirit is love, joy, peace, patience, kindness, goodness, faithfulness, gentleness, self-control; against such there is no law. And those who belong to Christ Jesus have crucified the flesh with its passions and desires. If we live by the Spirit, let us also walk by the Spirit.

Galatians 5:19-25   (Fourteenth Sunday after Trinity)

PREPARATION

From light cardboard such as file folder stock, cut two simple identical masks. For simplest design, make them of egg shape, cutting out only the eye-holes and the mouths.

For the one mask, turn the mouth downward to give a sad or depressed effect; for the other, curve the mouth upward, for a smile.

On the frown mask, write the words *angry, envious, jealous, gossiping, selfish, cheating, disobedient.* On the other write the words *loving, helpful, kind, generous, honest, obedient.*

This morning I'm going to show you my two faces. Actually, they're not really my faces at all; they are masks. But they are my faces, and yours, too. I think you'll see why.

Here is the first face. (Hold the frowning mask against your face, with the words away from the children.) This is the face of a person who lives just for himself. He always wants his way. But it's not a happy face, is it? Let's look on the other side to see what's really behind such a face. (Read, or have the children read, the various words.) Those are the sins we have when we live just for ourselves. It's what the Bible calls living by the flesh. But it's not a happy way to live.

That's why Jesus sends the Spirit to change us. The

opposite of living by the flesh is living by the Spirit of God. And that's this way. (Exchange masks.) This is a happy face, isn't it? Let's see why! Let's see what's behind this face. (Turn mask around, and have children read those words.)

Did you notice, this face is just the opposite of the other one. Where the flesh face said angry, the Spirit face said loving. (Go through all the words in the same way.) The difference is that this is the way we live by ourselves (holding up frowning face) and this is the way we live when Jesus sends his Spirit to us.

So, there's just one question. Would you rather live for yourself, or with the Spirit? That's not even hard to answer. We know! That's why Jesus came to us in the first place, to rescue us from living for ourselves. That's why he sends his Spirit to us. He gives us a new face.

Who Comes First?

SCRIPTURE

"No one can serve two masters; for either he will hate the one and love the other, or he will be devoted to the one and despise the other. You cannot serve God and mammon.

"Therefore I tell you, do not be anxious about your life, what you shall eat or what you shall drink, nor about your body, what you shall put on. Is not life more than food, and the body more than clothing? Look at the birds of the air; they neither sow nor reap nor gather into barns, and yet your heavenly Father feeds them. Are you not of more value than they?

Matthew 6:24-26   (Fifteenth Sunday after Trinity)

PREPARATION

Collect several textbooks, preferably those which nearly all of the children will be studying, such as arithmetic, language arts, reading, social studies. You will also need a checkbook and a Bible. If possible, conceal the Bible during the first part of the message, or just do not have it in the other stack of books.

Most of you know what these are, I am sure. (Allow children to answer.) That's right; they are schoolbooks. And they're very important, aren't they? Let's just look at them.

Here's an arithmetic book, and we couldn't get along without arithmetic. That's important. And here is a reading book. That's important too. This is a language book, to help us write to each other and talk to one another. That's very important. All of these books are, and if we have these, that's just about all we need.

Well, not really. Here is another book which is very important, and I'm sure your fathers and mothers will agree. (Show checkbook.) Now we have everything we need, don't we?

That's the way we often feel, and in fact, we often worry if we don't have all of these things. We get all upset if one or the other isn't as easy as it should be, or if we miss out on part of it, or if we don't have enough in this one. (Show checkbook.)

That's just the thing Jesus said people would do, but he also told them they could do something else. You see, there's one book missing from this stack, and that's this one. (Show the Bible.) Here is the book which tells us how much God loves us, and how he cares about us, and how he watches over us. He knows everything we need, and he is able to give it to us. That's even more important than all these other books put together.

That doesn't mean we have to throw these away. Not at all! But it does mean that we don't have to make them more important than they are. And it means that they will never come first with us. This one does that! Enjoy these, yes! Work with them, of course! But worry about them so that we forget God's care for us? Of course not! That's why this one is so important. It tells us God cares!

Building Our Muscles

SCRIPTURE

For this reason I bow my knees before the Father, from whom every family in heaven and on earth is named, that according to the riches of his glory he may grant you to be strengthened with might through his Spirit in the inner man, and that Christ may dwell in your hearts through faith.

Ephesians 3:14-17 (Sixteenth Sunday after Trinity)

PREPARATION

Since this will be a participation activity, there is no visual aid necessary.

It's good to see so many of you this morning, and to see how cheerful and healthy all of you are. That's something to thank God for, isn't it? Just think, he has made us all healthy and strong. In fact, he made us strong in two ways. He gave us strong bodies, and he gave us strong faith, too. With our bodies we can walk and run and play; with our faith we know Jesus is our Savior, and we know how much he loves us.

We talked about strong bodies. I wonder if I could have a strong boy help me this morning. Let's choose Steven. (Choose someone who is obviously a strong boy.)

Steven, will you show me your muscles in your arms please? (Indicate how you want him to show his biceps. Then feel them, making a comment about them.) But tell me Steven, how did your muscles get so big and so firm? (Allow him to answer, and continue from whichever answer he gives.) Suppose that you would decide never to do that again, and that you would never exercise these muscles again, what do you think would happen? (Again, allow time for his answer.) That's right, your muscles wouldn't stay as strong as they are, would they? They would get soft and weak, and we certainly wouldn't want that.

We said before that we have strong bodies and strong faith, too. Now, if our muscles get weak when we don't use them, what do you think happens to faith? That's right, it gets weaker, too. We can think about it like a muscle. Use it, and it gets strong, like Steven's biceps. (Flex your own muscles.) Forget it, and it gets weaker. (Let arms go limp.)

But Jesus doesn't want us to have weak muscles of faith, either. That's why God tells us that he will strengthen us through his Spirit in the inner man. When Jesus comes to us in his word, he is making us stronger people. When we read about him, or study about him in Sunday school or Bible class, he is building the muscles of our faith for us. When we worship together in church, or in our homes, or even alone in our bedrooms maybe, Jesus is giving his strength to us. He changes our weak muscles of faith into strong ones. (Flex muscles.) That's good news, isn't it? Jesus comes to live in us, and we can be strong Christians!

A Religion that Fits

SCRIPTURE

I therefore, a prisoner for the Lord, beg you to lead a life worthy of the calling to which you have been called, with all lowliness and meekness, with patience, forbearing one another in love, eager to maintain the unity of the Spirit in the bond of peace. There is one body and one Spirit, just as you were called to the one hope that belongs to your call, one Lord, one faith, one baptism, one God and Father of us all, who is above all and through all and in all.

Ephesians 4:1-6 (Seventeenth Sunday after Trinity)

PREPARATION

From light cardboard make a silouette or outline picture of a church. If it can suggest the general outline of your own building, so much the better. During the presentation you will also need a scissors.

Can anyone tell me what this building is? (Allow time for the response.) That's right, it's a church. Well, really, we ought to say that it's a church building. We know that people are the church, and buildings are just places people come to do what the church does. But this morning, let's think about this being the church, where people come who belong to Jesus. That's why it's his church.

But sometimes we forget that the church belongs to him. We seem to think that it belongs to us, and we can do with it as we like. We like a religion that fits us, and we even get angry sometimes if it doesn't.

One person says "I would like church better if the music were faster, and I won't come unless it is!" (Clip off part of the church.) Another says "I don't like the way we have worship, and I won't come back until it's changed." (Clip off another part.) "I don't like the preaching." (Clip another part.) "I don't like the people." (Clip more.)

We all like our own ideas and our own ways. But when we insist on them in the church, or stay away

103

unless we get them, what happens. Look what we have left. Is it a church now? Not like before, is it? But that's what happens when we get stubborn or angry or selfish about the church. Before long we don't have a church left.

That's why Jesus tells us that it is important for his people to live together in love for each other, in patience with each other, and in unity with one another. That means nothing is to separate us from each other. That's a lot to expect, though, isn't it?

But the good news is that Jesus doesn't expect something of us that he doesn't provide to us. Jesus brings us together with each other. He takes our sins of stubbornness and anger and selfishness and impatience, and he puts his love and forgiveness in their place. We have been baptized into the same faith, we have the same Lord, the same Father, the same Jesus, the same Spirit. Since Jesus has made us his people we have more to bring us together than to separate us. We don't need to make the church fit us; we have the power of Jesus, fitting us into his church.

Wind-up People

SCRIPTURE

I give thanks to God always for you because of the grace of God which was given you in Christ Jesus, that in every way you were enriched in him with all speech and all knowledge—even as the testimony to Christ was confirmed among you—so that you are not lacking in any spiritual gift, as you wait for the revealing of our Lord Jesus Christ; who will sustain you to the end, guiltless in the day of our Lord Jesus Christ.

1 Corinthians 1:4-8   (Eighteenth Sunday after Trinity)

PREPARATION

The visual aid for this message is a wind-up toy, preferably fairly large, which must be in working order. Before the message, be certain the toy is completely unwound, so that it will not function at all.

Isn't this a great car? I can really have fun with it. All I have to do is put it down on the floor and it will go all the way across the room. I know; I did it before. Just watch it move. (Place toy on floor, and watch it. It is not to be wound at this time.)

That's funny; I had so much fun with it before. I wonder what is wrong. (Allow children to respond. Undoubtedly someone will suggest that it needs winding.) Well, let's try that. (Wind the toy, place it on the floor so that it moves.) That's great! It works again! It just needed to be wound up!

Did you know that God's people are like that, too? We need to be wound up, in a way. Jesus made us his people when we were baptized, but we can't just coast along from that. And so he keeps re-winding us, whenever we share his word or receive him in holy communion.

That really gives us a good reason to be here every time we can, doesn't it? We might think we want to do something else, or let things get in the way. But this is the time that Jesus winds us up as his people again. We get run down, and he fills us with his love; we stop growing in our faith, and he gets us going again with his forgiveness.

Now, if you were a toy, would you rather be run down, or wound up? Which kind of Christian would you rather be?

Clean Clothes

SCRIPTURE

Put off your old nature which belongs to your former manner of life and is corrupt through deceitful lusts, and be renewed in the spirit of your minds, and put on the new nature, created after the likeness of God in true righteousness and holiness.

Ephesians 4:22-24 (Nineteenth Sunday after Trinity)

PREPARATION

You will need a doll with three sets of clothes, and a marking pen which will write on the clothes.

Some of you girls play with paper dolls, I suppose, and I imagine even you older girls did play with them. Of course, the boys probably don't, but Sally (hold the doll forward) has something to say to them, too.

You see, Sally was all dressed up one day to go shopping with her mother. She was just as nice and clean as could be. (Show Sally in her clean dress.) But while she waited, she found her brother's ink pen. Before long there was a smudge of ink here (make a mark) and here (make another mark) and here. (Make another mark.) And every time Sally tried to rub those marks away they just got worse. (Make some more marks.) She didn't know what to do.

But her mother knew. Of course she was sad that Sally had made her dress so dirty, and had messy hands and face. But she washed Sally's hands and face, and she went to the closet to get another dress, a nice clean one. (Change Sally's dress so that she is wearing the clean one.) Sally felt much better, but that's natural, isn't it. After all, if you had a choice of being dirty or clean when you go someplace, you'd want to be clean too.

And God tells us that's the way we are with our whole

selves, and not just with our clothes. He made us to be nice and clean, but we get ourselves all dirty with our sin. It's like making marks on our clothes. We disobey our parents, and there's the dirt of sin. (Make a mark on the dress.) We get angry with each other, and there's more dirt. (Make another mark.) We sleep in instead of getting up for Sunday school and church. (Make another mark.) If we wanted to make a mark for every sin, our clothes would be completely covered. In fact, they'd even be dirty without extra marks; that's the way we are. We are sinners.

But remember, Sally's mother didn't want Sally to be all dirty, and God doesn't want us to be all covered with sin, either. When we were baptized he gave us clean clothes and clean faces. (Put clean clothes on Sally again.) Jesus took our sins away and gave us his new white robe, as the Bible calls it. That's why he became a person just like us; that's why he lived, and that's why he died. He did it to take our dirty clothes of sin away, and to give us clean ones in their place. That's what happens when we receive him in his word or in the sacrament. He is giving us clean clothes.

Timmy Didn't Get Ready

SCRIPTURE

And again Jesus spoke to them in parables, saying, "The kingdom of heaven may be compared to a king who gave a marriage feast for his son, and sent his servants to call those who were invited to the marriage feast; but they would not come. Again he sent other servants, saying, 'Tell those who are invited, Behold, I have made ready my dinner, my oxen and my fat calves are killed, and everything is ready; come to the marriage feast.' But they made light of it and went off, one to his farm, another to his business, while the rest seized his servants, treated them shamefully, and killed them. The king was angry, and he sent his troops and destroyed those murderers and burned their city. Then he said to his servants, 'The wedding is ready, but those invited were not worthy. Go therefore to the thoroughfares, and invite to the marriage feast as many as you find.' And those servants went out into the streets and gathered all whom they found, both bad and good; so the wedding hall was filled with guests.

Matthew 22:1-10   (Twentieth Sunday after Trinity)

PREPARATION

Since this will be a story told without visual aids, there are no materials to prepare. Preparation will consist of developing familiarity with the story and making such adaptations as necessary to fit the time and place.

Do you remember the little boy we sometimes talk about? What is his name? (Allow children to answer.) That's right, it's Timmy! And this morning we have a Timmy and Tommy story.

Timmy's mother was going to take him to a movie one Saturday afternoon. It was a special cartoon feature, and Timmy really wanted to go. So Mother told him that they would go to the movie, and take Tommy, his best friend, when the work was done. He could hardly wait.

At lunchtime, though, mother told Timmy that she had to go to the store. But she told Timmy that as soon as she came home they would go, if Timmy had his toys put away, and took the papers out to the garage, and

109

put his roller skates and wagon into the garage, too. Timmy said of course he would do those little things, and his mother left.

But then guess what happened. Instead of picking up his toys, Timmy started playing with them. And he kept on playing and playing and playing. He forgot all about the papers, all about his roller skates, and all about the wagon . . . that is, until his mother came home.

Tommy came at the same time, and he was ready to go to the show. So was Timmy's mother, but Timmy was not. He wanted to do the work when he came home, but mother said he couldn't do that; it would be too late. She would just have to take Tommy, and Timmy would stay behind to do his work. It was a sad day for Timmy.

And really, we often seem to be much like Timmy. We get so interested in other things we forget all about Jesus. We get so busy we can't take time to learn about him, or to worship him, or to pray to him. That happens!

That's why Jesus told a story just like our story about Timmy. He wants his people to be ready for him whenever he comes. He came once to take our sins away, so we can be ready. And he comes to us now in his word, so that we stay ready. When we think we're too busy, we can remember that he is never too busy for us. With his wonderful forgiveness he takes away our busy-ness, and makes us ready. That's good news!

Ready for a Fight

SCRIPTURE

Finally, be strong in the Lord and in the strength of his might. Put on the whole armor of God, that you may be able to stand against the wiles of the devil. For we are not contending against flesh and blood, but against the principalities, against the powers, against the world rulers of this present darkness, against the spiritual hosts of wickedness in the heavenly places. Therefore take the whole armor of God, that you may be able to withstand in the evil day, and having done all, to stand. Stand therefore, having girded your loins with truth, and having put on the breastplate of righteousness, and having shod your feet with the equipment of the gospel of peace; above all taking the shield of faith, with which you can quench all the flaming darts of the evil one. And take the helmet of salvation, and the sword of the Spirit, which is the word of God

Ephesians 6:10-16   (Twenty-first Sunday after Trinity)

PREPARATION

Prepare a simple line drawing of a man in armor. (An easily followed illustration accompanies the Scripture passage cited, in *Good News for Modern Man*, The New Testament in Today's English Version, Second Edition, page 440.) Be certain to include the shoes, the shield, the helmet, and the sword.

Can anyone tell me what this man is doing? (Allow children to respond, encouraging them to give reasons for their answers.)

That's right; he's getting ready for a fight. He's a soldier from years ago, and he is wearing armor. Do you see it here on his feet, or on his arms, or even on his head? He's ready to fight!

But this is a picture of us, too . . . but in a different way. The Bible tells us that we are soldiers, too. We are soldiers for Jesus, and our enemy is the devil, who likes to make us sin.

This is the way we get ready for our fight. First, we have something on our feet. Let's call this armor the gospel, the good news that God loves us and that Jesus

111

has come to us. That gives us something to stand on. And here is our shield. We'll call that the shield of faith. When we know how much God loves us and that Jesus has done so much for us, we can be strong.

And here is the helmet. The Bible calls it the helmet of salvation, meaning that God has set us free from our sins. That protects us, too.

And see the sword. That's the sword of the spirit, the Bible says, and that is the word of God. When we have that we have protection . . . and when we have all this armor, we're ready to fight against sin and the devil. We'll have a lot of strength.

But do you know something? We're going to need that strength. We all do. Your mothers and fathers can tell you that no matter how strong we think we are, we just aren't strong enough. We need Jesus and all the armor he gives us.

So let's see again what he does give us. Here is the good news that he loves us. (Point to the shoes.) Here is the shield of faith. (Point.) Here is his forgiveness. (Point to helmet.) Here is the power of his word. (Point to sword.) And here we are, soldiers for him, ready for a fight. And do you know something else? We'll win! Jesus is on our side, and he already has won the fight for us.

We're Together

SCRIPTURE

I thank my God in all my remembrance of you, always in every prayer of mine for you all making my prayer with joy, thankful for your partnership in the gospel from the first day until now.

Philippians 1:3-5   (Twenty-second Sunday after Trinity)

PREPARATION

Place a large stack of books on one side of the room, using twenty large books or so. If possible place a small table on the other side of the room, to be a repository for the books.

I have work for someone this morning, so I would like a helper. Would anyone like to help? (Choose one.) Thank you, Richard, for offering to help. I'd like you to move that stack of books to this table. (Point to the books and the table.) Can you do that? Of course you can. But wait just a minute.

For Richard to move all those books by himself will take a long time, won't it. He'll have to make at least twenty trips. We could do it faster if we would each take one, couldn't we? Let's do it. (Allow the children to move the books.) Very good! All the books were moved so easily! We worked together! We were partners with each other.

And that's what the church is, too. The church is people who are partners with each other. It doesn't belong to the pastor or to the Sunday school teachers or to the ladies society or anything like that. It belongs to Jesus, as we have said before. And it's a place to be partners with each other in his work.

Of course, sometimes we don't like to be partners very much. Sometimes we like to have our own way, or not even do anything. Sometimes we get angry with one another and don't want to work with each other. But

113

just suppose that this morning Heidi had said "I won't carry a book at all!" and Don had said "If Heidi won't help, I won't either." Or think of what would have happened if Kathy had said "If I can't carry a blue book, I won't carry any." We would have quarrels instead of a partnership, and all we would see would be our sins against each other instead. That's the way the devil tries to break up the partnership in Jesus' church. He does it with our sins.

That's why the partnership in the church always starts out with Jesus. If we're going to be partners with each other, we have to be rid of those sins first. And that's what Jesus did for us. He came to be a partner with us, to take those sins away. When he suffered and died for us, and then came out of the grave on Easter he broke up the devil's hold on us, so that the devil can't break our partnership with Jesus or with each other.

And because we're really partners with Jesus, our partnership with each other can be fun. He fills us with his love, and that keeps the partnership going; he covers our sins with his forgiveness, and that keeps it going, too. He has even given us a partnership meal, in holy communion, and a partnership sign, in the sign of the cross. (Make the cross.) That's why I'm making the cross sign right now; it tells us we're partners . . . with Jesus, (make the vertical sign) and with each other. (Complete the cross horizontally.)

114

Two Flags

SCRIPTURE

Then the Pharisees went and took counsel how to entangle him in his talk. And they sent their disciples to him, along with Herodians, saying, "Teacher, we know that you are true, and teach the way of God truthfully, and care for no man; for you do not regard the position of men. Tell us, then, what you think. Is it lawful to pay taxes to Caesar, or not?" But Jesus, aware of their malice, said, "Why put me to the test, you hypocrites? Show me the money for the tax." And they brought him a coin. And Jesus said to them, "Whose likeness and inscription is this?" They said, "Caesar's." Then he said to them, "Render therefore to Caesar the things that are Caesar's, and to God the things that are God." When they heard it, they marveled; and they left him and went away

Matthew 22:15-22   (Twenty-third Sunday after Trinity)

(Note: This message can also be used in connection with national holidays.)

PREPARATION

If your auditorium has both a church flag and a national flag there need be no further preparation. If you cannot procure the two flags, make them from construction paper.

All of us know what this flag means, don't we? (Allow children to respond.) That's right; it means our country. This flag stands for us and for our land; it reminds us that we are people of our land. We even say a pledge of allegiance to the flag, because that means we are promising to be loyal to our country. We know that flag, all right.

And we know this one too, don't we? (Show church flag, permitting children to respond to it also. If they do not know the church flag, use this time for explanation of it.) Do you see this? (Point to cross.) This reminds us that Jesus has made us people of his country, the country we call the kingdom of God.

But which one do you think is more important? (Before children answer, you may wish to go on. If you

115

handle this as a conversation, be certain to ask for explanations too.) Some people say this one (point to national flag) is more important, since our country protects us, and gives us the freedom to worship. Others say this (point to church flag) is more important, since we want to love Jesus more than anything else. But do you know what God says? He says these are both important. Countries are important because they give us laws and government; churches are important because they give us the word of Jesus.

But God does say something else about them, too. He tells us we are to obey him rather than anyone else, and that even includes our country. If countries make bad laws, then our love for Jesus must come above them. But when our country has good laws, those good laws are for us to keep.

Maybe we'll have to solve our problem of two flags this way: This one (church flag) does come first, because Jesus does. But that helps us obey this one, too. (Point to national flag.) So it isn't one or the other, really. It's the two together because this one comes first. (Point to church flag again.) Jesus said "Give to Caesar the things that are Caesar's," and that's the government. (Point to national flag.) He also said "Give to God the things that are God's." (Point to church flag.)

He Makes Us Whole

SCRIPTURE

And behold, a woman who had suffered from a hemorrhage for twelve years came up behind him and touched the fringe of his garment; for she said to herself, "If I only touch his garment, I shall be made well." Jesus turned, and seeing her he said, "Take heart, my daughter; your faith has made you well." And instantly the woman was made well.

Matthew 9:20-22 (Twenty-fourth Sunday after Trinity)

PREPARATION

Divide a sheet of light cardboard approximately four inches by eighteen inches into four sections. (File folder stock works well.) Fold the cardboard at the section lines so that the first and last sections seem to form a four by nine inch cardboard.

In section one print the letters *sha* in large letters; in section four, print the letters *lom* in similar letters, so that the word *shalom* is formed when the card is folded together as directed above.

In the middle two sections print any words which describe how peace between people is broken. These words may include newspaper headlines about riots, war, thefts, etc., or they may be words such as selfishness, anger, jealousy, fear, envy, and others.

This morning we're going to review a Hebrew word which some of you may know. Or maybe you don't. Let's see. Here is the word. (Show the card.) Who knows what it is, or what it means? (Allow response.)

You are right, it's *shalom* and it means peace. But it means peace in a special way. It means peace because people are brought together, or because nothing separates them. It means completeness, or wholeness, just like my card. This is a whole word, a complete word. The letters are together. That's the word *shalom.*

But sometimes life isn't so peaceful. Things do separate us. (Open card so that the word is pulled apart.) Let's see what some of those things are. (Allow children to read, and if you like, comment briefly.)

But when these things happen we don't have peace, do we? We aren't together; we don't have wholeness. We might even say that we could put God on one side of this card, and we're on the other, with sins between us. Or we could say that we are one side, and other people are on the other, and again our sins are between us. (Hold card to illustrate.) We aren't together; we don't have peace.

And we never would have it, by ourselves. These sins are like being sick, and we just can't get over that sickness. But God didn't want his people to be sick with their sin-sickness, to be separated from him and from each other. So he sent Jesus to bring his healing to us. And that's just what Jesus did. He healed us by taking these things away. And he brought us back together again; together with each other, and together with God. (Bring sections of card together, so that the word *shalom* is obvious again.) This is what Jesus did for us, and this is what Jesus still does for us. We have been baptized into his *shalom*, his peace. He shares it with us when we hear the words of his forgiveness, or take his body and blood in the sacrament. We're brought back to God and to each other. That's not only a new word, though; that's a new life!

Here Is Jesus!

SCRIPTURE

"Then if any one says to you, 'Lo, here is the Christ!' or 'There he is!' do not believe it. For false Christs and false prophets will arise and show great signs and wonders, so as to lead astray, if possible, even the elect. Lo, I have told you beforehand. So, if they say to you, 'Lo, he is in the wilderness,' do not go out; if they say, 'Lo, he is in the inner rooms,' do not believe it. For as the lightning comes from the east and shines as far as the west, so will be the coming of the Son of man."

Matthew 24:23-27   (Twenty-fifth Sunday after Trinity)

PREPARATION

You will need four boxes, possibly of shoe box size or slightly smaller. In the first one place a picture of a large church building. In the second place several candy bars or lollipops. In the third place a picture of a large crowd of people, or simply a number such as 3246 IN CHURCH TODAY! In the fourth box place a cross and an alarm clock. Label each box with the words WE ARE THE TRUE CHURCH!

This morning we're going to hear about the church. We could expect that, couldn't we, since that's what we are. But we're going to hear something different. We're going to hear about people who claim to be the real and true church of Jesus.

That's actually what these boxes say, too. Each one of these is a church, let's pretend. And each one claims to be the best church of them all. Let's find out why.

Here is church number one. Can someone read what the label says? Right! It says: "We are the true church!" (Open the box.) And inside the box is a reason. (Show picture of the church building.) This one claims to be best because it has the biggest building.

Or let's look at this one. I wonder what is inside it. (Open the box and show the candy bars.) It says: "We are the best church because we give the best prizes for coming to Sunday school."

119

Here's church number three. Let's find out about it. (Show the crowd of people or the statement indicated in preparation.) This one claims to be the best church and the true church because it has such a large number of people.

Now, we'd better think about that for a while. Large buildings can be very fine. (Show the building.) And even prizes for Sunday school attendance might be all right. (Show them.) Certainly we like having many people to share Jesus' words with. (Show the crowd.) But to claim that these make a church the true church is wrong. In fact, Jesus even warned about such things. He called them false prophets.

So let's see what this box has in it. Well, that's simple enough! Here is the cross of Jesus! And that makes it the true church! It's not how big, or what prizes, or how many people, or anything like that! It's the forgiveness we have in Jesus.

But there's something else in this box, too. It's an alarm clock. Jesus said that he would be coming back again. That means we are to be ready, just like an alarm clock tells us to be ready to get up. That's part of the true church, too. We share the good news about Jesus who died for us on the cross, and who is coming back for his people.

So, what makes something a church? That's easy now. He does!

Where Do We See Jesus?

SCRIPTURE

Then the righteous will answer him, 'Lord, when did we see thee hungry and feed thee, or thirsty and give thee drink? And when did we see thee a stranger and welcome thee, or naked and clothe thee? And when did we see thee sick or in prison and visit thee?' And the King will answer them, 'Truly, I say to you, as you did it to one of the least of these my brethren, you did it to me.'

Matthew 25:37-40 (Twenty-sixth Sunday after Trinity)

PREPARATION

Collect several pictures of Jesus, representing different styles, or different artists. Collect also a set of pictures of people in various circumstances, all difficult. Suggestions: people in poor housing sections, or in an automobile accident, or hungry people, or war victims, refugees, etc.

How good are you at recognizing people from pictures? Shall we see? Who is this? (Show picture of Jesus and then wait for an answer.) Or, who is this? (Show next picture.) And how about this? (Show third picture.) Good! These pictures are all different, but we recognize Jesus, don't we!

Now let's look at some more pictures. How about this one? Who is this? (Allow the children to identify the pictures, answering freely. They will probably identify the events, but you can help the identification to reach a more personal level by simply adding that these are people who are in an accident, a grandmother without food, etc.) That was easy, wasn't it? We recognize people in these pictures, and Jesus in these. (Indicate the proper set as you speak.)

But do you know that Jesus said he is in these pictures, too. He told his disciples that even when they gave a glass of water to someone who was thirsty they were giving it to him, or when they gave food to someone who was hungry, they were giving it to him, or when they gave clothing to someone who needed it, they were giving it to him. (Use pictures to demonstrate.)

That makes it different, doesn't it? We think about Jesus this way, and we like to help him and show our love to him. But Jesus says to think of him this way, and that means to help and love him this way, too. And if we don't help these (hold up the pictures of people) we really are saying that we won't help him. (Hold up a picture of Christ.)

That's why we need Jesus ourselves. He came to be our helper. He came to open our eyes so that we can see him, both ways. And he came to fill us with his own love, so that we can share it with others.

And that's what our life is to be. It's a life of loving Jesus wherever we see him, this way (show his picture) or this. (Show picture of people.) And then when he comes back he can say to us, too "Truly, I say to you, as you did it to one of the least of these my brethren, you did it to me."

We're Ready

SCRIPTURE

"Then the kingdom of heaven shall be compared to ten maidens who took their lamps and went to meet the bridegroom. Five of them were foolish, and five were wise. For when the foolish took their lamps, they took no oil with them; but the wise took flasks of oil with their lamps. As the bridegroom was delayed, they all slumbered and slept. But at midnight there was a cry, 'Behold, the bridegroom! Come out to meet him.' Then all those maidens rose and trimmed their lamps. And the foolish said to the wise, 'Give us some of your oil, for our lamps are going out.' But the wise replied, 'Perhaps there will not be enough for us and for you; go rather to the dealers and buy for yourselves.' And while they went to buy, the bridegroom came, and those who were ready went in with him to the marriage feast; and the door was shut. Afterward the other maidens came also, saying, 'Lord, Lord, open to us.' But he replied, 'Truly, I say to you, I do not know you.' Watch therefore, for you know neither the day nor the hour."

Matthew 25:1-13 (Twenty-seventh Sunday after Trinity)

PREPARATION

You will need two flashlights, one with good batteries, and the other with either dead batteries or with no batteries at all.

I have two flashlights in my hands this morning, and I think you can see they're both very nice flashlights, aren't they? Now, if I were going to take two of you camping with me tonight, which flashlights would each one want. Suppose Robert and Richard were going with me. Robert, which flashlight would you want? (Allow him to pick.) Then, Richard, I'll give you this one.

But now let's ask something. Which one has the better flashlight? Robert, try yours. Does it work? And Richard, let's try yours. (React according to whichever one has the working flashlight.) Oh, oh . . . that's a real problem. Here we are, all ready to go camping, and your flashlight won't work. We're really not quite ready, after all. We have to get some batteries!

And Jesus told his people a story something like that, only he talked about oil and lamps, since they didn't have flashlights and batteries in those days. But the idea is the same. He wants his people to be ready when he comes back.

Now, if I want to I can put new batteries in this flashlight very quickly. But if I needed the light in a hurry, it wouldn't be very good to have to run to the store first to get some. It would be better to keep the batteries charged up all the time. (Turn on the good light.)

That's true for God's people, too. Jesus would like us to have charged-up batteries of faith all the time. We do that through sharing his word, and receiving him in communion. Jesus comes to us now to keep us ready. He makes us ready to live with him now, and ready to live with him forever. So, why have burned out batteries (turn on switch in nonworking light several times, displaying some impatience) when he will keep us ready?

Forgiveness Makes It a Home

SCRIPTURE

. . . and be kind to one another, tenderhearted, forgiving one another, as God in Christ forgave you.

Ephesians 4:32 (Mother's Day)

PREPARATION

You will need a fairly good size cardboard box, preferably one which opens from the top, and which has both top flaps intact. The box will represent a house, with the flaps for the roof. Staple or tape a white sheet of paper on the front, and sketch a door and two windows with a marking pen. You may wish to draw a few lines for the boards and bricks on the front, and for the shingles on the roof. (This sketching is not at all necessary, although it does add to the effect.)

Inside the house place a little piece of brick or stone, a small piece of wood, an item or two of doll house furniture, a paper doll man, woman, and child. Also, include two hearts cut from red construction paper, and a cross.

Today we're going to play "Let's Pretend" for a little while. You see, I have a cardboard box here, but I've tried to make it look like something else. I tried to make it look like a house. But maybe it's not enough like one, so we'll just have to pretend.

In fact, let's pretend that this is our own house, and we want it to be a good one. So, maybe we should find out what makes a house something special, something nice, something good.

It could be the way the house is made, perhaps out of this. (Take out piece of brick.) Or maybe it's made of this. (Take out the piece of wood.) Or maybe, since we all enjoy nice furniture, that would be the thing.

Or perhaps it's the people of the house who make the home something special . . . the father, and the mother . . . and the children. (Take out the figures separately as you speak.)

But we can have all of those things, and our house

still might not be what we want it to be. We really need something else. (Take out the first heart.) And that something is love. Love makes a home a pleasant place.

But we know that sometimes even in our homes, things happen to our love. We get angry with each other. (Crumple the heart slightly.) Or we show that we are jealous of one another. (Crumple the heart more.) Or we don't listen to Mother, or don't obey Father; we don't show our love. (Crumple the heart completely.) It's too bad, but that's what happens, and when it does, home isn't so pleasant anymore.

That's why we really need something else. (Hold up the cross.)

Of course, we don't need just the cross. We need Jesus, who came to bring God's love to us, and to bring us back into God's family. He came to bring us forgiveness through that cross. With it he takes our crumpled hearts, and makes them new again. (Put the crumpled heart back into the box as you begin talking about the cross. With this last sentence, take out the new heart.)

That's why we need Jesus to make our houses something pleasant to live in. His forgiveness makes it a home. It's something he gives to us, and we can give to each other.

We Often Forget

SCRIPTURE

Bless the Lord, O my soul; and all that is within me, bless his holy name!

Bless the Lord, O my soul, and forget not all his benefits.

Psalm 103:1, 2 (Thanksgiving Day)

PREPARATION

You will need ten pennies to hand to children who come forward. Privately request one of the children beforehand to forget to thank you when he receives his penny.

(If it is possible, this message can be presented even more effectively if you can give each child a penny. It is still necessary to make the necessary arrangements before the service with the one, though.)

God has given us so much to be happy about, that today I want to show you how happy I am by sharing something with you. I have ten pennies in my hand, and I'm going to give those to you. (Pass out the pennies, paying no particular attention to whether the children respond with thanks. Give the child whose help you enlisted the last penny.)

Very good, but did anyone notice that Mark didn't say a "Thank you?" I wonder how he could forget such a thing. Mark, how could you forget it? (Have Mark answer that you had told him not to respond with thanks.)

That's right, I asked Mark not to say "Thank you." I know that he is a very polite young man, and that he would say "Thank you." But I wanted him to show us all what we are like sometimes. You see, we can remember to thank someone else for a penny, but we forget to thank God for all the things he gives us. I wonder if anyone thanked him for the air we breathe, or for the water we drink, or for the clothes we wear. It's too bad that we forget, isn't it?

So, it's good to have a Thanksgiving Day, to remember that God never forgets us. He has even given us something better than air or water or clothes. He has given us Jesus. That's the way he remembered us especially. He remembered us with his forgiveness, even for our forgetting. That's why we can be thanksgiving people. Jesus has taken our forgetting away, and he gives us a new sense of being thanking people.

So, remembering that, you may go to your places now . . . and today you may even keep the pennies I gave you.

(As the children walk back, wait just briefly, and then make whichever response is appropriate.)

How about that! They remembered to say "Thank you!"

or

How about that! They forgot to say "Thank you!"